GW01605834

Jennings in Particular

This Armada book belongs to:

*Other titles by Anthony Buckeridge in Armada*

Jennings Goes to School
Jennings' Little Hut
According to Jennings
Take Jennings for Instance
Thanks to Jennings
The Trouble with Jennings
Trust Jennings

# Jennings in Particular

Anthony Buckeridge

First published in this new (revised) edition in 1972
by William Collins Sons & Co. Ltd., London and Glasgow
First published in Armada in 1976 by William Collins
Sons & Co. Ltd., 14 St. James's Place, London SW1A 1PF



Printed in Great Britain by
Love & Malcomson Ltd.,
Brighton Road,
Redhill, Surrey.

# CONTENTS

CORIN

*his book*

CHAPTER 1

# *Roof-top*

THE WICKET was three lines chalked on the wall of the bicycle shed. At the other end of the pitch, a pull-over flung down on the tarmac marked the bowling crease. The bat was frayed at the bottom like a worn paint brush, and the old tennis ball had lost its bounce during the four terms it had lain lost in the long grass behind the gymnasium.

Though the equipment was primitive, the atmosphere was tense on the field of play . . . For the first time in history a World Cricket XI was playing a test match against a team from Outer Space.

At first glance there seemed to be little physical difference between the human beings of the "home" side and their visitors from beyond the radiation belts. All had the usual number of arms and legs; all spoke the same language at the tops of their penetrating voices. Indeed, an onlooker might well have thought that a group of third-formers of Linbury Court School were enjoying a scratch game of cricket in the half-hour before the dormitory bell.

Yet things are not always what they seem; and on closer inspection a keen observer might have noticed certain clues enabling him to tell which of the players were Earthmen and which were cricketing creatures from worlds beyond our own.

For example, Jennings fielding at cover point for the alien team could well have been taken for a lively eleven-year-old English schoolboy. It was only when one observed the elastic band stretched round his scalp from which two ball-point pens sprouted like antlers that one realized that here, surely, was a native of the planet Mars!

Or take Darbishire, for instance, standing at the bowling crease polishing his glasses with a dock leaf while he waited for the game to start. He certainly *looked* like a human being with his fair hair, mild blue eyes and faintly hesitant manner.

And then one noticed the green, plastic vegetable colander that he wore on his head. Here, without doubt, was the clue to his identity. As Darbishire himself would have been ready to explain, anyone knowing that green plastic vegetable colanders were normal headgear in the outer reaches of the solar system would have guessed at once that the wearer must be a player from the planet Pluto.

Atkinson (from Jupiter) and Venables (from Venus) made up the rest of the four-man side from outer space. The former wore an extra eye drawn on his forehead with blue crayon; the latter, having no physical marks to display, gave proof of his Venusian upbringing by talking in the idiom of a Redskin in a television Western.

"Me, mighty famous Space-pace bowler. Me hit

Earthman's middle stump with Unplayable Flying Object," he announced, as Temple arrived at the wicket to open the innings for Earth.

But Jennings as captain of the fielding side had other ideas. "You can't take first over," he told the representative of Venus. "I'm putting on Darbishire to open the bowling."

"Darbishire! You must be off your runners!" Venables was so outraged by his captain's choice that he relapsed into standard English to register his protest. "Old Darbi can't get a ball within a hundred miles of the wicket. He's about as much use as a clockwork orange. He only bowls sneaks or wides."

"He bagged first over when I won the toss. I can easily take him off if he makes a mess of it," Jennings explained.

"I shan't make a mess of it," Darbishire assured them. He had finished polishing his glasses and was now polishing the flabby tennis ball in the hope that he would be able to make it spin. "We outer-space chaps know all about crafty bowling. We've been listening to B.B.C. commentaries ever since radio telescopes were invented."

So saying, the expert from Pluto shouted, "Play!" and ran six paces forward to deliver the first ball in this unusual series of test matches. But as his arm swung upwards the green plastic vegetable colander slid forward over his eyes. The ball shot off at a tangent and caught Atkinson, fielding at square leg, a glancing blow on the shoulder.

At the other end of the pitch the batsman relaxed his stance. "Wide!" he announced, unnecessarily.

"Sorry about that, Temple," Darbishire apologized. "It's the gravity down here on earth. It's different where I come from, and it puts you off."

The space-man removed his green plastic helmet and, making full allowance for the gravitational pull of the earth, delivered his next ball. This time he caught his foot in the pullover marking the bowling crease and his aim was no truer than before.

"Wide!" Temple said again as Atkinson retrieved the ball from a clump of nettles. "If we go on like this we shall make a hundred without even touching the ball."

"It's all Jennings's fault—putting old Darbi on to bowl," Venables complained. "Everybody knows Darbishire's cricket is pathetic. Everybody knows he plays like a flat-footed starling."

In fairness to Darbishire it must be admitted that Venables's protest was not based upon personal observation. It is unlikely that Venables had ever watched starlings playing cricket; and even if he *had*, it is doubtful whether he would have noticed much resemblance between Darbishire's prowess at the game and that of some member of the feathered team who happened to be suffering from fallen arches.

Even so, there was a ring of truth in the criticism that Jennings could not ignore. "All right then, I'll take him off at the end of this over if he doesn't bowl any straighter," he agreed.

But Darbishire never even finished his over. His next delivery, to everyone's surprise, pitched well down the wicket and in line with the stumps. Temple stepped forward and smote it with all his strength.

It was a beautiful stroke. The ball rose up over the heads of the fielders gaining height with its momentum. For a second it seemed about to soar right over the roof of the gymnasium which marked the boundary on the leg side of the tarmac "field." Then it lost height, hit the balustrade above the gutter and bounced to rest on the flat roof of the building.

The test match came to an abrupt halt.

"Hooray! Boundary six!" shouted Temple, waving his bat round his head like a tomahawk.

"No, it isn't. You're out! Full toss on to the gym roof is 'out'," Atkinson protested.

"It wasn't full toss. It hit that drain pipe thing first."

"Ah, but it didn't come down again. It's a lost ball."

"That proves I'm right then," Temple insisted. "You look up the laws of cricket. You always get six for a lost ball."

"Only if you've got another one to go on playing with," said Jennings. "You can have your six runs if you like, but that's your lot. Unless somebody's got a spare ball we could borrow, the game's over."

It seemed a tame ending to a match which had started off with such high hopes less than two minutes before, and as no spare ball was available it was natural that some of the players should feel strongly about the way in which the fixture had been mismanaged.

"It's all Jennings's fault. Trust him to go and make a carve-up of it," said Atkinson. "He tells us it's the most important match in the history of the solar system——"

"Ah, yes, but you've got to use your imagination," Jennings broke in. "Everybody knows you don't *really* have cricketers from Jupiter and Mars and places."

"Not yet, we don't, but we might one day. And think what would happen if they went and put you in charge of it." Atkinson continued, as fresh possibilities of the scheme occurred to him. "Supposing in, say, twenty years' time the M.C.C. invited well-known space athletes to come hundreds of light years to play a test match at Lords. You wouldn't expect the game to fizzle out in the first over, just because nobody on Earth had remembered to have a spare cricket ball handy in case of accidents."

"That's crazy," said Darbishire, rallying to his friend's support. "We don't even know if there are people in outer space, let alone whether they play cricket."

Atkinson pointed an accusing finger at the discarded vegetable colander. "Well in that case, Darbi, why did you have to go cavorting about with that thing on your head. It was you who said they wore space helmets like that on Pluto."

"But that was when we were just pretending. Surely

you can see the difference between—" Darbishire tut-tutted and shook his head. The argument was becoming so confused between fact and fiction that there was no point in going on with it. And indeed, a diversion occurred at that moment for Martin-Jones, a tail-end batsman for the All-World XI, returned from making a quick inspection of the kitchen garden on the far side of the gymnasium.

"There's a chance of getting the ball back if we're quick about it," he reported. "I thought perhaps it had gone over the roof and rolled down the other side, so I went to have a look."

"And had it?"

"No, it must still be up there; but old Robo's been painting the drainpipe round the corner and he's gone off and left his ladder there."

It was a chance too good to be missed. The flat roof of the gymnasium was known to be the last resting-place of scores of balls which had vanished over the parapet and had never come down again. Normally, the only way on to the roof was through an attic skylight, but as the attic was locked and out of bounds there was never much hope of reclaiming lost property by this route. But if Robinson, the school cleaner and odd-job man, had obligingly left a ladder pointing the way aloft it would be folly not to take advantage of it.

They would have to be careful though. Climbing ladders and scaling roofs was clearly forbidden by school rules. Furthermore, the far wall of the gymnasium marked the boundary of the school vegetable garden and this, too, was territory where boys had no business to be.

"Come on then," said Venables. "What are we waiting for?"

There was a general movement towards the gymnasium, but Jennings called them back.

"It's no good everybody going," he pointed out. "Old Wilkie's over by the tennis courts and he'd spot it at once if everyone suddenly vanished off the face of the earth." He glanced round the group. "Temple and I can go up and get it while you others pretend you're still playing cricket."

"Why me?" Temple demanded.

"Because you hit it."

"All the more reason for someone else to go and fag it, then. Batsmen don't have to do their own fielding. It's your team's job to look for lost balls."

"That's right," Martin-Jones agreed. "Send old Darbi up. It was his fault for bowling an easy one. Temple couldn't help hitting it."

"Well, I like that," the bowler complained. "Just because I sent down a beautiful, straight——"

"Don't argue, Darbi. We'll be better off on our own," Jennings broke in. "Just you and me, eh!"

There was a comfortable, easy-going friendship between Jennings and Darbishire, despite the fact that in appearance and temperament each was quite unlike the other. Jennings was impulsive, wide-eyed with curiosity and eager to play a leading part in whatever aspect of school life happened at the moment to catch his fancy. Darbishire, on the other hand, was content to be an onlooker—or rather, he *would* have been content, had he been given the chance. But, as Jennings's constant companion, he became so involved in his friend's activities that he often found himself thrust into situations for which his cautious nature had little appetite.

The present situation was a case in point.

"It's jolly risky going up on the roof without per," he demurred as Jennings led the way round the corner of the gymnasium. "Old Sir's got photo-flash eyeballs. He's only got to glance over here and——"

"He can't see through brick walls," Jennings pointed out. "Lucky for us old Robo's painting the other side first."

The gymnasium at Linbury Court was a detached building lying back from the main school block from which it could be reached by a covered passage-way. For most of its length the building was single-storied, but at one end a staircase led to a passage which, in turn, gave on to a small storage attic with a skylight at roof level.

Once round the first corner the boys were out of the duty-master's line of vision, though they had to trespass in the kitchen garden to reach the ladder, which they found leading up to the roof as Martin-Jones had described. Fresh wet paint overhead showed that the odd-job man had been working on the gutters and drain-pipes, but as there was no sign of him, or of his paints and brushes, it seemed reasonable to assume that he had finished work for the day.

Jennings hurried to the foot of the ladder and scampered aloft like a monkey up a mainmast. Darbishire proceeded with caution. He was not at his best on ladders, and by the time he was half-way up the cabbages in the kitchen garden seemed a long way below. He stopped for a moment and a little wave of giddiness swept over him.

"Come on! Don't just stand there like a half-baked potato," Jennings called down from above. "And mind the wet paint when you step off at the top. I've got a great splodge of it all down my shirt."

Darbishire gripped the rungs tightly. It was all right if you didn't look down, he told himself. Or was it that you shouldn't look *up*? Better not to look anywhere at all, he thought; and with an effort of will he started climbing again, his eyes staring at the wall ahead, his fingers flexed, his mind a blank.

He felt better when he reached the top and Jennings helped him off the ladder on to the roof. "It took you long enough to get here," his friend said impatiently.

Darbishire nodded. He wasn't going to let Jennings know how nervous he had felt. "I was—er—admiring the view," he said.

"Never mind the view. We've got a job on." Jennings turned his back on the scenery to begin the task on hand and at once his eyebrows shot up in surprise. "Wow! Look at this lot, Darbi. It's like a pirates' treasure trove."

The flat roof of the gymnasium was a sort of charnel-house of lost balls. They lay about the zinc-coated surface in dozens; tennis balls, cricket balls, rubber balls, golf balls—even an odd football or two. Judging by their condition some of them must have been there for years. Every spherical object hit, kicked or thrown high enough to reach the roof but not high enough to pass right over it, lay before them like wrecks awaiting salvage.

Jennings collected half a dozen balls, stuffed them inside his shirt and made his way across the roof to the parapet facing the playground. Down below he could see Venables, Temple and the rest of the players staring up expectantly.

"Got it?" demanded Temple.

By way of reply, Jennings hurled the old tennis balls over the balustrade and stood grinning with glee as a scramble for possession started down below.

Darbishire arrived with two composition cricket balls and a perished football bladder as Jennings went back to the middle of the roof for further supplies. Then, for some minutes, they amused themselves by bombarding their friends with all the lost property that had ever come to rest upon the roof. In addition to the balls they found two box-kites, five model gliders and an old gym shoe.

None of the property was of any value after suffering from so much exposure; but for the boys on the roof it was fun to take aim at the groundlings below and watch them first dive for cover as the balls came down, and then dart out during a lull to rescue some punctured ball or battered glider which they feared had been lost for ever.

Soon the roof was stripped of its debris and the pockets of the boys on the playground were bulging with salvage.

"That's the lot," Jennings called down. "We've got enough balls now to play fifty thousand test matches." He turned away, and as he did so a whistle blew in the distance. At the first sound Jennings stopped short, dropped on his knees and pulled Darbishire down behind the low balustrade.

Mr. Wilkins was on duty that evening, and the whistle was his signal that break was over. In the excitement of the bombardment Jennings had forgotten all about Mr. Wilkins. Had he seen them from the tennis courts? They must have been obvious skyline targets standing there on the roof, if the master had happened to glance in the right direction.

"D'you think he saw us?" Darbishire quavered.

Jennings shrugged. "We'll soon know. He'll be coming over to chivvy the other chaps indoors. We must have been mad standing in his gunsights like that."

"We've got to get down quick! The dorm bell will be going in five minutes," said Darbishire. On hands and knees he started to crawl back across the roof, but Jennings restrained him.

"It's too late. Old Wilkie might see us going down. Our best plan is to wait here till they've all gone indoors, and then fox in after them through the changing-room window."

Darbishire had little enthusiasm for his friend's best plan. It was bad enough having to face that ladder again even if Mr. Wilkins *hadn't* spotted them. And if, on top of that, they had to go crawling through windows and dodging the duty master at every step of the journey, the prospect was horrifying.

"I wish we'd never come up here," he mumbled. "I wish we'd left the rotten old ball to stay lost."

"Ssh! Stop nattering, Darbi. You don't want old Wilkie to know we're up here. He's already heading this way by the sound of it."

The warning of Mr. Wilkins's approach was unnecessary, for the duty master had a voice like a loud-hailer, and could be heard booming out orders and instructions as he made his way round the school grounds.

"Come along now, you boys, hurry up indoors!" he ordered, striding across the pitch of the ill-fated interplanetary test match.

Jennings and Darbishire crouched lower as his voice floated up. "Quickly now, Venables! What's all that nonsense you've got stuck up your pullover?"

"Only a few lost balls, sir," came the reply from below.

Jennings stiffened, wondering whether the master was going to press for details. But apparently all was well, for with a grunt of disapproval Mr. Wilkins went on: "Well, take them out and put them somewhere else. You're ruining the shape of your clothes." There was a pause, and then: "What on earth have you got plastered all over your forehead, Atkinson?"

"That's my extra eye, sir," Atkinson replied proudly. "We were playing a famous outer-space test match, you see, and I was the bug-eyed monster from Jupiter. Everybody on Jupiter has three eyes, sir—so far as we know."

"Do they indeed!" It was clear from his tone that the duty master had little interest in bug-eyed cricketers from beyond the Van Allen radiation belts. "Well, make sure you wash that horrible daub off your face when you get to your dormitory."

Then the sounds at ground level died away as boys and master made their way indoors. When all was quiet, Jennings rose to his feet and said: "Come on, then! Coast's clear. If we go straight away we may get inside before they lock the door."

Darbishire gulped. Apart from the risk of being found out, he still had this other worry preying on his mind: the light was failing now, his pulses were pounding—and somehow or other he had got to nerve himself to climb down that wretched ladder!

"You go first, Jen," he whispered as they crossed the roof. "I'll hold the top steady while you go down, and then you stand on the bottom rung and watch my feet for me."

"Righto!" Jennings reached the parapet ahead of his friend. "Only don't hang about admiring the view, this time. We've only just got time to——"

His words tailed off; and when he spoke again his voice was shrill with dismay. "Hey, Darbi, quick! Look what's happened!"

Darbishire hurried forward still trying to decide which was the safest way of going down the ladder. Then he looked over the parapet and saw that his problem no longer existed.

The ladder wasn't there any more!

CHAPTER 2

# *Refuge*

THE EXPLANATION was simple. Mr. Henry Robinson, known out of earshot as old Robo, had worked as a cleaner and odd-job man at Linbury Court for long enough to have learned that boys were creatures to be viewed with mistrust.

They would walk over his highly-polished floors, making dirty wet trails from leaking tins of paint water; they would leave live tadpoles in the wash-basins or dead grass snakes in other people's gumboots; they would wedge wet socks behind radiators or seal up the nozzles of fire extinguishers with sticky toffee. Never on purpose, of course, they would assure him: these perfectly natural actions were always the result of absent-mindedness or curiosity. All the same, they were enough to keep old Robo constantly on his guard in his dealings with the younger generation.

The ladder was a case in point. Robinson finished his day's painting just as the boys were coming out on to the playing field for evening break. He cleaned his brushes and stored his paint tins, and was just about to sit down for his evening meal when he remembered that he had left the ladder propped against the gymnasium wall.

In theory, it should be safe enough where it was until the morning, he thought. It was out of sight and out of bounds so far as the boys were concerned. And then his cautious nature warned him that you couldn't be too careful. Better be safe than sorry, and remove all signs of temptation from their paths.

So he made his way back through the vegetable garden and took the ladder down just as Jennings and Darbishire were bombarding their friends with old tennis balls on the far side of the roof.

Robinson's forethought was no consolation to the prisoners on the roof as they stood staring over the parapet at the thirty-foot drop below.

"What's happened! What on earth are we going to do?" cried Darbishire.

"It's obvious what's happened," Jennings said testily. "We'll have to shout for help and hope somebody hears us."

"But that means we'll be caught. And if old Wilkie finds out that we came up here without per——"

"He's bound to find out some time—either now or to-morrow morning."

"To-morrow morning!" Darbishire was appalled at the prospect. "You mean we've got to stand shivering on this roof *all night*!"

"Unless we shout for help. There's no other way of getting down, so far as I can see."

They shouted for help with the full force of their lungs, but their cries went unheeded. By now the whole school were indoors consuming milk and biscuits in the dining-hall at the far end of the main block. And after that they would be going up to the dormitories, out of sight and out of earshot. The chance of rescue seemed slim.

Suddenly, Jennings said: "Hey, Darbi! What about that skylight into the attic. Perhaps we could get in that way."

Darbishire shook his head. "The attic's out of bounds," he said reprovingly.

"Well, so is the roof if it comes to that. We couldn't be any worse off, wherever we were."

"Yes, but the door's locked. If we got in through the skylight we still couldn't get out on to the staircase."

"How d'you know it's locked? I bet you've never tried it," Jennings said with rising hope. "For all you know it's only bolted on the inside, and if we can get in through the window all we've got to do is to slide the bolt back and——"

"All right then; let's go and try."

They made off across the flat roof heading for the skylight at the far end. When they had gone half-way, Darbishire spotted a serious flaw in his friend's argument.

"Hey, just a mo, Jen," he said coming to a sudden stop. "If the door's bolted on the inside as you say, how could the chap who bolted it have got out again?'

Jennings hadn't thought of that. "Over the flat roof and down a ladder," he hazarded.

"But that's crazy. Why should he want to do that?"

"I didn't say he *wanted* to do it. I said he *could* have done."

"But then nobody else could——"

"Oh, don't natter, Darbi," Jennings broke in impatiently. "We don't know whether the door's locked, bolted, barred or guarded by Alsatians until we've been in and had a look. Supposing it wasn't locked after all! A proper couple of Charleys we'd look, if we stayed out here and then found it was open all the time."

He led the way to the skylight, a frosted-glass window a yard square enclosed by a wooden frame projecting a few inches above the level of the surrounding zinc.

Jennings took hold of the lower edge of the window and tugged. To his delight it yielded slightly, but it was too heavy for him to raise upright without help.

"Grab hold of the other corner!" he ordered.

Darbishire took the strain and heaved, and between them they prised the window open on its rusty hinges. As it rose, Jennings noticed that the catch had snapped off on the inside. "Lucky old us!" he said, nodding at the broken fitting. "We'd never have got in otherwise."

Darbishire pulled a long face. "Lucky! It'll be time to talk about being lucky when we've got out of this jumbo-jet of a hoo-hah."

They peered down through the opening and saw the bare boards of the attic ten feet below. Jennings went first, letting himself down to the full stretch of his arms, then dropping lightly to the floor.

Darbishire, a poor gymnast, needed help, so Jennings clutched the flailing legs and guided his friend's descent. Then they rushed to the door and Jennings seized the knob.

It was useless. The door was locked.

"Oh, fish-hooks, this is frantic," Darbishire moaned as their last hope of escape dissolved in despair. "And it's not even any good shouting for help now. If they couldn't hear us before, they couldn't possibly hear us from here."

This was certainly true, for the little store-room over the empty building was the farthest point from the main block which could be reached while still remaining within the school precincts.

A worried look spread over Jennings's face and he turned and glanced up at the skylight. "Perhaps we ought to climb back on to the roof and try shouting again from——"

There was a resounding crash from overhead.

The heavy window which they had left unsupported in its upright position had fallen back into its frame. It had taken the combined strength of both boys to raise it when they had been able to move freely. For one of them to attempt it alone, while perched wobbling on the shoulders of the other, was clearly out of the question.

"That's that, then," Jennings said in a flat, resigned voice. "We'll have to stay here until somebody finds us."

The attic in which they were imprisoned was a store-room for the camping kit of the school's scout troop. Pinned on the walls were flags and patrol emblems, coloured posters of wild birds and a diagram showing how to tie clove hitches, bowlines and sheepshanks. On the back of the door hung the motto, *Be Prepared*, and the Scout Law inscribed in large gold letters on a green board. There were tents, groundsheets, billy-cans, blankets and buckets—everything needed for a night under canvas. The only snag was that the dingy attic, ten feet square and festooned with cobwebs, was hardly an inviting camp site.

"We can't stay here all night," Darbishire protested. "Besides, what's old Wilkie going to say when he finds we're not in the dormitory with the others?"

Perched on upturned buckets, they discussed their predicament. Their biggest worry was the fact that nobody knew where they were. Venables and his friends, unaware that Robinson had made off with the ladder, would assume that their cricketing colleagues had descended to earth and gone indoors with the rest of the school. Even when they failed to appear in the dormitory their absence would be loyally concealed from the duty master for as long as possible on the grounds that the missing boys were probably engaged in some unlawful exploit of their own choosing.

And would Mr. Wilkins notice they were missing? So far as he knew they might well be in Matron's dispensary, receiving first-aid treatment for mosquito bites or blistered heels, when he went into Dormitory 4 to say good night and call silence! If this happened, the chances of being rescued before morning were slight indeed . . . No milk and biscuits to-night, no comfortable bed; perhaps no breakfast next day either. Whatever punishment was finally meted out would be trivial compared with the ordeal they would have to undergo before their release.

Finally, Jennings said: "It's no good getting in a panic. If we've got to stay in this Black Hole of Calcutta all night we might as well make ourselves comfortable."

He rose from his bucket and inspected the camping equipment stacked on the shelves. On the top shelf he found a green, fleecy-lined sleeping-bag fitted with a zip-fastener, so he took it down and unrolled it on the floor.

"This'll stop me catching frostbite, anyway," he said. "You'd better find something to wrap yourself up in. It'll be like a deep-freeze in here by three o'clock in the morning."

Darbishire selected a couple of moth-eaten army blankets. He sorted through a stack of equipment in the vain hope of finding a pillow, and finally decided to make do with a canvas bucket instead.

"There's just about everything here that we need and yet it's no good to us!" he said disgustedly, indicating the shelf behind him. "Look—a hurricane lamp, but no matches, a frying pan, and no bacon to cook in it. There's even a compass to find our way back to civilization—only we can't get through the door!"

Jennings tried to cheer his friend's flagging spirits. "Hey, look at this," he said, taking an old oilskin sou'-

wester from a hook and putting it on (he had long since discarded the ball point pens and elastic band so fashionable on Mars). "How about this for launching the lifeboat, eh?"

The humour was not appreciated.

"Oh, shut up," Darbishire said irritably and stooped to unroll his blankets. "Here we are up to the eyebrows in the most frantic hoo-hah since the Battle of Hastings and you have to make feeble Form One jokes."

Jennings shrugged. "Better than moaning, anyway." The sou'wester was several sizes too large for him and the brim came down well over his eyes. "It'll keep my head dry in case the roof leaks," he said, knotting the tapes beneath his chin.

Then he opened the sleeping bag and wriggled himself inside. Lying on his back he took hold of the tag and tugged the zip-fastener shut, right up to his chin.

A few moments later, Darbishire heard his friend fidgeting and muttering to himself in exasperation. "What's up, now?" he demanded.

"It's this stupid zip," Jennings complained. "When I pulled it up just now, I got the front of my shirt caught in it, and now I can't budge the thing one way or the other, however hard I try."

Darbishire snorted. "Huh! Is that all! I should have thought we'd got enough trouble on our plates without worrying about feeble zip-fasteners." He was tired, hungry, miserable, and very worried indeed. The light was fading now, but as he lay bundled in his blankets he could just make out the gold lettering of the Scout Motto on the back of the door.

The advice it offered wasn't much help just at the moment, Darbishire thought, as he wriggled his head about on the unyielding canvas bucket. It was all very well saying *Be Prepared*, but with a beetle-headed clodpoll like old Jennings in charge of the proceedings, how could anyone tell what to be prepared for next?

* * * *

It was not until they were in their pyjamas and ready for bed that the occupants of Dormitory 4 gave any thought to the absence of two of their number.

Then Venables, sitting on his bed lassoing his toes with his dressing-gown cord, said: "What's happened to ye famous spacemen from Mars and Pluto? Old Wilkie will go into orbit if they haven't made Earthfall before he comes in to call silence."

Atkinson bounced on his bed like a clown on a trampoline. "They didn't come in for milk and biscuits," he observed between bounces.

"Perhaps they've beetled off down to old Jennings's tuck-box," suggested Temple. "Perhaps the Head caught them and carted them off to the study for ye famous spine-chilling treatment."

"And perhaps he didn't," Atkinson retorted. "They'll turn up soon. They must be about somewhere."

Nobody was worried at this stage. But when Mr.

Wilkins came in a few minutes later on his tour of the dormitories, the situation took a turn for the worse.

Mr. Wilkins was a large, bustling man with a brisk manner and a short supply of patience. Though fond of the boys in his care, he persisted in viewing their behaviour through adult eyes and, as a result, could never understand the antics of the rising generation.

"Everybody in bed?" he boomed as he clumped into the room like a drill squad marking time in army boots. He glanced at the two empty beds. "Where are Jennings and Darbishire?"

Venables, Temple and Atkinson looked up with puzzled frowns as though unaware, until that moment, that their friends were not amongst those present. They exchanged innocent looks like crafty witnesses for the defence concocting an alibi. Loyalty demanded that Mr. Wilkins's suspicions should be allayed.

"Jennings and Darbishire, sir?" echoed Venables with the air of one trying to recall names that were vaguely familiar. "Yes, they're—er—they're not actually here just at the moment, as you might say, sir. I think they're probably—er—somewhere else, so to speak."

Dormitory 4 was a small room furnished with five beds, three washbasins and a clothes cupboard. There was nowhere for anyone to hide, but even so Atkinson had a good look round, even peering under the beds and behind the cupboard before reporting his findings.

"No, they're definitely not in here, sir—I've checked," he said.

"I can see they're not in here, you silly little boy," Mr. Wilkins retorted. "Get up off your knees and get into bed at once."

"They might be up in the dispensary, sir," Temple suggested. "Matron's running a new line in rather decent cough mixture and——"

"They're not in the dispensary—I've just come from there," Mr. Wilkins broke in. He glanced at his watch. It was nearly time to call silence. "If those silly little boys aren't in bed in two minutes from now, I'll—I'll—well they'd better look out."

He strode from the room to see whether the absentees were dawdling about on the lower landing. They were not! Neither were they in the bathroom, nor trespassing in someone else's dormitory. Worried now, Mr Wilkins widened his search to cover the less likely hideouts. He looked behind the bootlockers in the tuck-box room, and even glanced behind the piano in the music room, though reason told him that no boy could squeeze into a recess only four inches deep!

It was nearly fifteen minutes later when he arrived back in Dormitory 4, and by now he was very worried indeed.

"This is ridiculous," he fumed. "They're nowhere in the building at all. Are you *sure* you boys don't know where they've got to?"

"No sir," said Dormitory 4 in chorus. And, by now, they were all as puzzled as Mr. Wilkins.

"There's only one thing for it then," the duty master

decided. "I shall have to get the headmaster to phone the police and report them missing."

The police! Venables, Temple and Atkinson exchanged uneasy glances. It was one thing to fob Mr. Wilkins off with unlikely excuses when their friends were merely trying to dodge him on the back staircase; but it was a different matter if the police were to be called in. This was no longer a game. This was serious.

"Well, sir, we know where they were when you blew the whistle for 'all-in'," Venables said hesitantly. "They were—er—on the roof of the gym, sir."

"They were *where!*" Mr. Wilkins was horrified.

"But we thought they'd come down again. You see we were playing cricket——"

"Cricket! On the *roof*?"

"No sir, down on the tarmac. It was a Test Match you see——"

"Earth versus Outer Space, sir," Atkinson reported. "Jennings was a famous Martian, and I was a bug-eyed Jupiterian and Venables was——"

"Quiet, boy!" snapped Mr. Wilkins. Interesting though the subject might be on some other occasion, this was hardly the moment, he felt, to listen to a detailed description of the players from the planets. "What in the name of thunder were they doing on the roof?"

"Fetching the ball, sir," Venables informed him. "You see Robinson had left a ladder there and——"

"Had he indeed! That explains a lot." Mr. Wilkins

glared at his informants. "And I suppose they were up there just over my head when I was sending you boys indoors for milk and biscuits?"

"Yes, sir."

"Doh!" With an effort Mr. Wilkins controlled his feelings. "Why didn't you tell me all this before?"

"You didn't ask us, sir. You said, did we know where they were and we honestly didn't because we thought they'd come down and——"

"All right, all right." Now that he had a clue to work on, Mr. Wilkins hurried out of the dormitory and took the stairs two at a time. It was almost dark now, and if those silly little boys were still marooned thirty feet above ground level, the sooner they were brought down in safety the better.

He'd need a torch, of course! Only that morning he had confiscated a handsome specimen from Rumbelow who had been practising Morse code flashing under the lid of his desk while waiting for the mathematics lesson to begin. Pausing only to collect the torch from the master's desk in Form 3 classroom, Mr. Wilkins made his way out through the side door and across the tarmac playground to the site of the short-lived test match.

Flashing his torch, he stared up at the parapet of the gymnasium and called: "Jennings! . . . Darbishir ! Are you there?" But the only answer was the echo of his own voice.

Then he went round to the far side of the building and saw that the ladder had gone. Were the silly little boys still up there hiding from him, or had they come down before the ladder had been removed? He must find Robinson and make a thorough inspection of the roof, without delay!

With this in mind he set off across the kitchen garden, heading for the odd-job man's cottage, but on the way he almost fell over the ladder, laid out on the ground by the tool-shed wall.

This should solve the mystery one way or the other! For a moment he hesitated wondering whether he could manage without help, but as there was no light in the cottage he decided to carry on alone.

Mr. Wilkins was powerfully built. Heaving the ladder upright, he swung it across his shoulder and carried it back to the gymnasium and set it against the wall.

When he reached the roof he flashed his torch around but there was no sign of the boys—and no answer when he called their names.

Mr. Wilkins was baffled. They couldn't possibly have got down after the ladder had been removed. So where on earth . . .?

Then he remembered the attic with its skylight opening on to the roof. Why, of course! They might well have taken refuge in there and then found the locked door barring their escape.

Now he knew where they were, he must decide on the best way of releasing them, he thought, as he crossed the roof. Ladders could be dangerous in the dark, and getting the boys down in safety might be something of a problem.

Mr. Wilkins reached the skylight and swung the window up with a mighty heave. "Jennings! . . . Darbishire!" he called into the darkness below . . . Still there was no answer. Puzzled, the master shone his torch into the interior.

Then, like Darbishire an hour earlier, Mr. Wilkins found that the problem now facing him was not the one he had been worrying about.

The attic was empty!

CHAPTER 3

# *Rescue*

THERE WAS NEVER any doubt that the remaining members of Dormitory 4 would rally to the aid of their friends.

No sooner had the door slammed behind Mr. Wilkins than Atkinson sat up in bed and said: "Wow! Poor old Jen and Darbi. They won't half stop a fast one when old Sir's megaton missile goes pinging off the launching-pad. Pity we can't rescue them from his gruesome clutches."

"Perhaps we can if we're quick about it," Venables suggested. "*If* they're still out there on the roof, that is: it all depends on that."

"How? We haven't got a helicopter," said Temple.

But Venables's plan needed no helicopter. As a keen tenderfoot in the Peewit patrol he had on several occasions been into the scout troop's store-room and knew about the window in the roof.

"If we went into the gym and beetled up the stairs we could get into the attic," he explained. "Then we could let them in through the window and they'd be home and dry while old Wilkie's still running round looking for them."

"H'm. *Sounds* all right." Atkinson frowned in thought. "But isn't it locked?"

"Yes, but I know where the key is," Venables told him. "I saw Mr. Carter putting it back in the cupboard at the top of the stairs after we'd been in there tidying the kit."

Temple grinned. "That takes care of that, then. And I bet old Wilkie doesn't know where the key's kept because he never takes Scouts. He'll look a proper Charley when he comes round again and finds them tucked up in bed."

With any luck it seemed likely that a rescue operation would have every chance of success. But speed was essential if Mr. Wilkins was to be outwitted.

Venables was the obvious choice to lead the expedition as he knew where to find the key. He would need someone to help him to open the window, he decided; although lacking the experience of Jennings and Darbishire he had no idea how difficult a task this might turn out to be.

"I'll come and help you," Temple volunteered. "What about security, though. Supposing we meet a master!"

"We shan't if we go right away," Venables assured him. "They're all having their supper—except old Wilkie of course." They'd have to keep an eye open for the duty master, he reminded himself. They could only guess at his movements and hope that their guesses were right. It was a risk, but a risk worth taking.

"Come on, then," Venables went on, groping under his bed for his slippers. "We'll be there and back while Sir's still running round looking for Robo's ladder, if we're quick."

Atkinson escorted the members of the break-out gang as far as the landing. "Good luck," he squawked in a voiceless whisper as the conspirators tiptoed down the stairs pulling on their dressing-gowns as they went.

There was no one about as they crossed the hall and let themselves out through the side door. All was quiet, too, as they pattered down the covered passage for (though they had no means of knowing it) Mr. Wilkins was, at that moment, stumbling over Robinson's ladder on the far side of the kitchen garden.

Tense with excitement the two boys reached the outer door of the gymnasium. The door was never fastened at that hour of the evening, for it was not until he had finished his supper and read the paper that Robinson made his round of the outbuildings to see that each was secured for the night.

The staircase was a tunnel of darkness as Venables and Temple groped their way up. At the top, Venables ran his hands along the wall until he located the cupboard. The store-room key was hanging on a nail just inside, and in a matter of seconds his fumbling fingers had found it and he was leading the way along the corridor to the door at the far end.

"All right so far," the leader assured his companion. "The only snag will be getting old Jen and Darbi off the roof and in through the skylight."

As he spoke Venables inserted the key in the lock, but even before he had turned it a voice called out from the other side of the door.

"Hey," said the voice. "Who's that out there?"

"It's me—it's us," Venables called softly.

"Who's me—who's us?"

"Venables and Temple. Who's that in there!"

"Me—us. Jennings and Darbishire."

"What are you doing in the attic? You ought to be out on the roof," Venables complained. "We've got the key. We've come to rescue you."

"Well get on with it then, instead of making speeches through the door panels." The speaker was Darbishire and there was no mistaking the tone of urgency in his voice. "For goodness' sake hurry up! We've just about had a basinful of this gruesome old hole."

Venables opened the door. The moon was just beginning to rise and a pale shaft shone down through the window overhead. By its light the rescuers could see Darbishire hopping from foot to foot with relief just inside the door. At first they couldn't see his companion, until their attention was attracted to a shapeless, faceless bundle half-sitting, half-lying on the floor at the far end of the room.

The bundle wriggled forward to greet them. It was Jennings, his face obscured by the sou'wester, his arms and legs pinioned inside the sleeping bag.

"Come on, Jen. Don't waste time fooling about," Venables said in a brisk whisper. "Old Wilkie's on the prowl, looking for you two. You've just got time to get into bed before they start phoning the police, if you come right away."

He turned to lead the way back to the staircase with Temple at his heels and Darbishire trailing just behind. Jennings, however, made no effort to follow.

"Hey, don't go off and leave me," came in tragic tones from beneath the sou'wester.

The trio stopped and wheeled round in surprise.

"Come *on*, Jen, for goodness' sake," Temple said impatiently. "There's no time to muck about. There isn't a second to lose."

"I'm *not* mucking about," Jennings protested. "I can't walk—that's all."

"Can't *walk*!" Temple was anxious now. "You mean you've broken your leg or something?"

"No, but I can't get out of this sleeping bag. I can't even get my arms free. I've gone and zipped everything up together inside."

They came back to help him, but there wasn't much they could do. In tugging the sliding-clip up to his neck, Jennings had caught not only the top buttonhole of his shirt but also the dangling tapes of the sou'wester, knotted under his chin. As a result the zip was jammed fast with a wedge of material which no amount of pulling or pushing would ever set free.

"This is hopeless," Venables complained after half a minute of wasted effort. "You must be bonkers, Jen. Whatever did you want to do it for?"

"I didn't *want* to do it! It was an accident." Jennings defended himself. "You don't think I'd go and truss myself up like this just for my own selfish pleasure, do you?"

"Stop arguing and let me have a go," said Temple. He took hold of the tag on the sliding-clip and tugged with all his might, but again the clip refused to budge. "It's the tapes on this crazy hat that are holding it," he decided. "We might stand more chance if we got that off first."

Seizing the brim behind the ear-flaps, he tried to pull the sou'wester forward over the victim's head. Once more he was foiled by the ends of the tapes caught up in the zip and succeeded only in forcing the headgear down over Jennings's face, blotting out his vision and muffling the sound of his voice.

Venables danced with impatience. "Oh, for goodness' sake! Old Wilkie will be heading this way in two bats of an eyelid. He's bound to think of the attic sooner or later."

In this, Venables was correct; for even as he was speaking, Mr. Wilkins was raising the head of the ladder to the parapet at the far end of the building.

Suddenly Darbishire said: "I know how to get him free."

They turned to him with rising hope. "How?"

"Get a pair of scissors and snip the stitches——"

"But we haven't *got* any scissors you clueless clodpoll," Temple broke in.

"No, I know. I was just wishing we had."

"Well, stop wishing! We haven't got time to go and get any with old Wilkie breathing down our necks."

Temple turned to the prisoner in the sleeping bag. "You'll jolly well have to get back to the dorm under your own steam, Jen, and we'll try and get you free when we get there."

The journey down the stairs, along the covered way, in through the side door and up three flights to Dormitory 4 was one which Jennings was to remember for a long time to come.

Anyone who has ever taken part in a sack race will know that there are two approved methods of reaching the winning post. The first is for the competitor to stretch his legs apart, push his feet into the bottom corners of the sack and waddle along like a penguin. The second method is to keep the feet together and proceed by leaps and bounds, taking care not to trip over the folds of the sack festooned about the ankles.

There are other ways, of course: one can lie flat on one's back and roll like a log, or lie flat on one's face and arch the body forward like a caterpillar crossing a cabbage leaf. These latter techniques, however, tend to be frowned upon in the best sack-racing circles and are seldom encountered at well-organized athletics meetings.

Jennings made use of the first two methods in his journey to Dormitory 4. Supported on either side by Darbishire and Venables, he floundered along the corridor to the head of the stairs. Going down in the dark was a difficult proceeding, and he solved it by squatting on the top step with his feet two stairs below and bumping himself down in a sitting position.

"Phew! Blow that for a lark!" he complained when they reached the bottom and emerged from total darkness into the covered passage. Here, faint beams of moonlight showed the way ahead and the going was easier.

"How would it be if we carried him?" Temple suggested.

"Too heavy," objected Darbishire. "And it would take longer really, because we'd have to keep stopping to change arms. I only wish we'd got a trolley or a bath chair or a——"

"Oh shut up, Darbi! You need your brains testing. Wishing for scissors! Wishing for trolleys! You sound like Cinderella's godmother: you'll be wishing for a glass coach drawn by white mice if you go on much longer." Venables sounded rattled as the group made its way along the passage. "Get a move on for goodness' sake. At this rate we'll find old Wilkie waiting for us when we get back to the dorm. He may even be there already."

This time, Venables's conjecture was wrong—but not seriously so. As the boys hurried in through the side door, the duty master was shining his torch down into the attic which they had left two minutes and forty-three seconds earlier.

The trek upstairs was a nightmare for Jennings and his companions, even though the landing lights were on to guide them on their way.

At first, Jennings tried using the same method in reverse that had enabled him to descend the staircase in the gymnasium: but bumping himself up took longer than bumping himself down, so on the second flight he stood upright and jumped one step at a time, with Darbishire and Temple supporting his elbows. Progress along the landing was easier, but for the uncertainty of not knowing whether or not they had raced Mr. Wilkins.

Their doubts were dispelled by Atkinson staring goggle-eyed in amazement over the banisters as they came up the last flight.

"Wow! Fossilized fish-hooks. What on earth are you doing in that sleeping-bag, Jen?" he greeted them.

"Never mind what I'm doing. Where's Sir?" Jennings demanded.

"I haven't seen him. He hasn't been back here."

"Phew! Thank goodness." Jennings reached the top step and floundered towards the unlighted dormitory like a seal on an iceberg. He collapsed panting and gasping on the bed, while Darbishire searched through his sponge bag by torchlight for his nail scissors.

"What's happened? What's going on?" Atkinson persisted, but no one had the time or the patience to pay any attention to his queries.

Darbishire's nail scissors were so blunt that they would hardly have pierced the skin of a rice pudding, let alone the stout material in which the metal strings of the zip-fastener had been stitched.

"I can't see what I'm doing with this feeble old torch," he complained. "We'll have to put the light on."

"Too risky. Old Wilkie would see it," Venables decided. "We'll just have to hope that he doesn't——"

He broke off as a door slammed down below in the hall and the sound of heavy footsteps came wafting up the stairs and in through the open dormitory door.

"Wow! Sir on the scent! We don't want him marching in here now," he went on. "Get into bed, Jen, and pull the blankets up."

"How do you think I can do that with my arms in the bag!" Jennings protested.

"Well, do *something*. And Atki, you nip out on to the landing and try and head Old Wilkie off. Tell him they're both in bed, so he needn't bother any more."

As a rule it was Jennings who took charge of a situation, Jennings who gave the orders. This time it was Venables: and the fact that he could take command, even temporarily, without a word of protest from the natural leader was proof of how deeply Jennings's morale had been shaken by the events of the last few minutes.

Atkinson pattered out on to the landing and called down over the banisters: "Sir! Oh, sir. There you are, sir! It's all right. Everything's under control."

The heavy footsteps stopped at the first landing. "What d'you mean, 'everything's under control'?"

"Jennings and Darbishire, sir. They're in bed, sir. Tucked up between the sheets ever so nice and snug, sir. They were just a tiny bit late coming up, that's all."

"Were they indeed!" From the tone of his voice it seemed unlikely that Mr. Wilkins would leave the latebedders to stay snugly tucked up for the rest of the night.

"Yes, sir. They—er—they got delayed. But you needn't bother any more because they're asleep now. Or rather——" Atkinson was doing his best, but there was no point in over-playing his hand. "Well, maybe not actually *asleep*, but they're pretty drowsy, so if I were you, sir——"

"You tell those two boys to report to me in the staff room immediately," Mr. Wilkins boomed in a voice of thunder.

"But, sir . . ."

"At once, do you hear! At once! Tell Jennings and Darbishire, awake or asleep, that if they're not in the staff room in one minute from now, I shall—I shall—" The duty master waved his arms in the air trying to think of a spine-chilling threat suitable for the occasion. Somewhat lamely, he finished up: "Well, they'd *better* be in the staff room in one minute from now—or else!"

Atkinson returned to the dormitory. "You heard," he said.

CHAPTER 4

# *Retribution*

When Mr. Wilkins reached the staff room a few moments later he found his colleague, Mr. Carter, seated in an armchair reading the evening paper.

Mr. Carter, the senior assistant master, was as different from Mr. Wilkins as rhyme from reason. Where Mr. Wilkins was excitable, Mr. Carter was placid—a friendly man, calm in the midst of chaos. Where the former was baffled by the behaviour of growing boys, the latter had a deep understanding of their needs and would lend a sympathetic ear to any eleven-year-old beset by troubles of his own making.

Mr. Wilkins strode into the staff room and slammed the door behind him.

"I've just about had enough trouble from those silly little boys in Dormitory 4—and from Jennings in particular," he complained as he flopped heavily into an easy-chair. "He and Darbishire have been up on the gym roof looking for lost balls, if you please."

"Really!" Mr. Carter sounded interested. "And did they find any? There must be dozens of old——"

"I don't know whether they found any and I don't care," Mr. Wilkins broke in irritably. "That isn't the point. What concerns me is that I went up on the roof looking for them, and they weren't there."

"And where were they?"

"I don't know yet, but I soon shall," Mr. Wilkins replied. "I've just given Messrs. Jennings and Darbishire exactly sixty seconds to report to me to explain their conduct."

He glanced at his watch and at the same moment there came a knock on the door. It was the timid, half-hearted tap of a visitor who was not looking forward to the reception awaiting him.

"Come in!" roared Mr. Wilkins.

The door opened to reveal Darbishire hopping nervously on the threshold. He was wearing a dressing-gown to conceal his day clothes, but the effect of being roused from sleep was marred by his socks and outdoor shoes, plainly visible below the hem of his disguise.

"You—er—you told me to report to you, sir," he said.

"I told you *both* to report to me," Mr. Wilkins corrected. "Where's Jennings?"

"He's—er—I think he's just coming, sir. He's on his way now."

As though in proof of this statement, loud thumping noises could be heard coming along the corridor from the direction of the stairs.

The noise was difficult to identify. In the distance it resembled the rumble and thwack of a busy evening at a ten-pin bowling alley: but as it drew nearer it sounded more like a kangaroo chasing a wallaby across the Australian outback.

Mr. Wilkins shot out of his chair like a rocket from its launching-pad. "What—what—what on earth is that horrible hullabaloo?" he demanded. Crossing the room in three strides, he swept past Darbishire into the corridor. Mr. Carter followed at a more leisurely pace.

Then, the two masters stood staring at the approaching figure as though it was some biological specimen hitherto unknown to science: the eyes and the top of its head were visible, but the lower half of its face was covered by a waterproof hat worn in the style of a horse's nose-bag.

The creature had no external limbs. From the neck downwards the body was encased in a green cocoon, hanging in concertina-like folds where it touched the floor.

It was not easy to tell what species the creature belonged to. Indeed, if it resembled anything at all, it looked like an Egyptian mummy practising for the hundred-and-twenty yards hurdles.

Mr. Carter winced and said: "Oh *no*! Not Jennings again!"

But Mr. Wilkins had more to say. "Doh! I've never in all my life—! What in the name of thunder are you doing, boy. Get out of that ridiculous bag immediately!"

"I can't, sir," the mummified figure confessed. "The zip's got jammed."

"Eh! Of all the nonsensical tomfoolery!" Mr. Wilkins strode forward and took hold of the tag and tugged; but he only succeeded in pulling the prisoner off balance so that his feet slid from under him and he collapsed in a helpless bundle on the floor.

"What did you want to get into the thing for in the first place!" Fuming with indignation, the master lifted the boy on to his feet. "I tell you to report to me, and you come bouncing down the stairs like a pre-packaged sack of potatoes. I've never in all my life——"

"The first thing to do is to get him out," Mr. Carter suggested. "The explanations can wait until afterwards." He inspected the zip-fastener and went into the staff room in search of scissors.

A few minutes later, when the stitches had been cut and the buttonhole disentangled from the tapes of the sou'wester, Jennings stepped out of his fleecy container with a sigh of relief. "Oh, thank you, sir. Thank you *very* much, sir. Thank you very much *indeed*, sir," he said to Mr. Carter. "I thought I'd have to stay in it all night, and it was so hot inside I thought I should either boil or melt or——"

"Quiet!" snapped Mr. Wilkins who was not interested in Jennings's comfort or in his chemical reactions to high temperatures. "I want to know why you boys were on the gym roof, and where you've been and what you've been doing."

But again Mr. Carter intervened. He took Mr. Wilkins into the staff room and behind the closed door suggested that the hour was too late to hold an inquiry into the why's and wherefore's of the evening's misadventures. The boys would have to be punished, of course, but that, too, could surely wait until the morning.

Mr. Wilkins looked at his watch and agreed. After all, he hadn't yet had his supper. He opened the door and barked instructions to Jennings and Darbishire to go to bed at once and report to him after breakfast the following day.

The culprits turned and made their way up the stairs, Jennings with the sleeping bag slung over his shoulder. As they went, they could hear Mr. Wilkins complaining to Mr. Carter about the stupidity of boys in general—and of Jennings, in particular.

"It's fantastic! They must be off their heads," he was saying in exasperated tones. "Every time I'm on duty those silly little boys in Dormitory 4 manage to reduce the routine of the school to a shambles of chaos and confusion. Believe it or not, Carter, I left them playing a perfectly harmless game of cricket on the quad, and less than half an hour later——"

His voice died away as the staffroom door shut with a slam.

* * * *

There was a variety of punishments awaiting Jennings and Darbishire when they reported to Mr. Wilkins after breakfast the following morning. These included losing points for their "House" and detention on the next three half-holidays. This last imposition was more severe than it sounded, for it meant that they would not be able to go on the junior picnic planned for the following Saturday week.

Furthermore, Mr. Wilkins announced that he proposed confiscating the salvaged tennis balls and throwing them on the bonfire so that no one should profit from the roof-top escapade. In this he was not entirely successful, for the word got around and some of the contraband mysteriously disappeared before it could be gathered in.

"Mouldy chizz about the picnic," Darbishire complained to his friend as they left the staff room after Mr. Wilkins's lecture had run its course. "We'll be the only ones left behind in Form 3."

"Never mind. We'll find something to do," Jennings said vaguely. . . . In the light of what actually happened on Saturday week his prophecy was something of an understatement!

The juniors' picnic held during the first half of the summer term was, on this occasion, supervised by Mr. Carter and Mr. Wilkins. The headmaster, Mr. Pemberton-Oakes, was not keen to go with them, for the last time he had attended he had sat on an ant-hill and been plagued by wasps buzzing round his sandwiches at every bite.

"I suggest, Carter, that you take them down by the river near Dunhambury," Mr. Pemberton-Oakes said to his senior assistant in the staff room on Monday evening when they were discussing the outing. "I'll get Matron to see that the food and things are ready soon after breakfast, and you can all get away on the ten o'clock bus."

Mr. Carter consulted his list. "What about Jennings and Darbishire?" he asked. "Wilkins insists on their staying behind as a punishment."

"Ah, yes, of course. That business on the roof!" The headmaster thought for a moment and said: "I don't see that Jennings and Darbishire should present any problems. I'll find some occupation to keep them out of mischief. An afternoon spent in weeding my garden might help to teach them the error of their ways."

The days passed. The weather was warm for early June and, when Saturday morning dawned, bright sunshine gave promise of a fine day to come.

At ten o'clock Jennings and Darbishire stood at the window of Classroom 3 watching their more fortunate colleagues gathering on the quad *en route* for the bus stop. Mr. Wilkins had set them enough work to last them the morning, but they were in no mood to settle down to arithmetical problems.

"I'm going to belt through those rotten old sums as fast as I can," Darbishire said, forcing himself away from the window. "Then, if there's any time left, I can get on with my stamps." Only that morning the latest issue of a monthly philatelic magazine had arrived for him by post and he was anxious to browse through it.

"You'll be lucky," said Jennings. "We may have got rid of old Wilkie for the day, but that still leaves Mr. Hind and all the other masters—including the Head.

I bet you what you like the Archbeako's sitting in his study planning some ghastly torture to keep us busy all afternoon."

Mr. Pemberton-Oakes was certainly seated in his study when Jennings was making his observation, but he was not thinking about the detainees in the classroom. Instead, he had the telephone to his ear and was listening to Miss Thorpe, a kindly, bird-like woman who devoted her energies to sponsoring worthwhile activities in the neighbouring village of Linbury. She it was who presided over the Women's Institute, organized jumble sales, supervised pre-school playgroups and packed the female inhabitants of the village into motor coaches to visit places of historic interest.

As usual when telephoning the headmaster, Miss Thorpe had a favour to ask. ". . . and as you know, Mr. Oakes, it's the church fête this afternoon. We usually hold it in July, of course, but this year we thought we'd have it earlier and as it's such a lovely day——"

Miss Thorpe had a high-pitched, penetrating voice not unlike that of a well-trained mina bird, and the headmaster removed the receiver to a more comfortable position nine inches away from his ear while he waited for the request which he felt sure must be coming. Surely she wasn't going to ask him to distribute the prizes again, he thought! He had undertaken that duty at the parish fête the previous year and, thanks to Jennings and Darbishire, the occasion was still fresh in his memory.*

* see *Just Like Jennings*

This time, however, the request was a simple one.

"We shall need more seating accommodation for the people watching the primary school's maypole dancing," Miss Thorpe trilled into the telephone. "And knowing what a lot of deck-chairs you have in your cricket pavilion, I wondered whether you would be good enough to lend us a dozen or two for the afternoon?"

"Certainly. Yes, of course. Only too pleased," said Mr. Pemberton-Oakes, relieved that she was asking for something so trivial. "I'll bring them along to the vicarage garden."

"That's so kind of you, Mr. Oakes, The dancing's arranged for after tea, so you needn't bother to bring them too early. And thank you *so* much. It's so kind of you to help us in this way."

"Not at all! Not at all! Delighted."

He had intended to go into Dunhambury during the afternoon in any case, the headmaster reminded himself as he replaced the receiver. He would get a couple of boys to collect the chairs and stack them on his trailer which he could leave in Linbury on his way through the village. He made a note on his jotting pad and returned to his work.

An hour later, Jennings laid down his pen and said: "Well, I reckon I've done enough sums to keep old Wilkie quiet when he comes back this evening. How are you getting on?"

Darbishire shook his head sadly. "I'm still stuck on the one about the cyclist going at eight miles an hour, and trying to get to the town before the bus overtakes him going three times as fast."

"That's a crazy sum! If he was in such a hurry, he'd leave his bike in the ditch and get on the bus when it caught him up." Jennings dismissed the problem with a wave of his hand. "Let's have a look at your stamp magazine and cheer ourselves up."

The most cheering item of news in the *Junior Philatelic Bulletin* was an announcement of a forthcoming issue of British postage stamps commemorating famous scientific inventions of the twentieth century.

"Wow! I'd like some of those." Jennings peered over his friend's shoulder at the illustrations reproduced on the first page. "When are they going to be on sale?"

Darbishire did some research amongst the small print below the illustrations. "June 16th," he announced. "If we could buy some and have them postmarked on the very first day they come out, they might be worth hundreds of pounds in a few years' time."

"*Hundreds* of pounds?" Jennings was incredulous.

"Well, perhaps not hundreds—but quite a lot. More than a few pence, anyway. But they've got to be posted on the day of issue or it doesn't count."

Jennings produced his diary and thumbed through the pages. Then he said: "D'you think they'll be on sale at a titchy little post office like Linbury Stores?"

"They're bound to have a few," Darbishire assured him. "Of course, if you want to be sure of getting some you'd jolly well have to be one of the first in the queue."

"That's the snag," said Jennings. "June 16th is a Monday and we'll be going into school just after the post office opens. On the other hand," he went on thoughtfully as further possibilities occurred to him: "On the other hand, it means that none of the other chaps in the school will be able to get any either, so if we put my plan into operation they'll be worth even more because they'll be so rare."

"Your plan?" queried Darbishire in puzzled tones. "You mean you've thought out a way of getting down to the post office when everybody else is in school?"

"Not yet, I haven't," Jennings admitted, thrusting his diary into his pocket. "But I've got plenty of time to work one out between now and June 16th. I'll think of something, Darbi; you see if I don't!"

CHAPTER 5

# On Target

MR. PEMBERTON-OAKES had at first intended to keep Jennings and Darbishire busy weeding his garden for the best part of the afternoon. But, mindful of his promise to Miss Thorpe, he decided shortly after lunch to transfer their energies to a task of more immediate purpose.

At half past two he let himself in through his garden gate, just as Jennings was chasing Darbishire round the rose beds, and showering him with handfuls of old grass clippings. The showers ceased as the boys looked round and saw that they were no longer alone.

"Come here, you two," the headmaster ordered. Then he said: "As you don't appear able to carry out my instructions without being watched all the time, you can come and do a little job where you're less likely to get up to mischief."

The folding canvas chairs were in the pavilion, he told them, and his car with the trailer already attached was standing on the quad. Two dozen chairs were to be collected and loaded on the trailer in a tidy fashion. Assuming they could count up to twenty-four, he inquired with heavy irony, was it asking too much to hope that they could carry out this simple task without wrecking the trailer or leaving the pavilion looking as though it had been hit by a bomb?

They thought they could do this. "Yes, sir. Of course, sir. We'll be ever so careful," Jennings assured him.

Half an hour later when the headmaster came out on to the quad, he had no fault to find. The trailer was neatly stacked with deck-chairs and the willing workmen were standing beside it waiting for further instructions.

The headmaster thought for a moment. Miss Thorpe would probably appreciate some help in setting the chairs out in the vicarage garden. He himself could not stay to do this as he had another appointment, but that was no reason why Jennings and Darbishire should not continue to make themselves useful.

He opened the car door and said: "Jump in! We're going to take this load to the parish fête."

The boys were delighted. This promised to be a better way of spending the afternoon than stuffing fistfuls of lawn clippings down each other's necks.

They were still, of course, convicted felons serving a sentence and the headmaster left them in no doubt about their status as he drove along the road to the village. "When you have set the chairs out and Miss Thorpe has no further need of you, you will come straight back to school," he said.

"Do you mean walk back, sir?" Jennings asked.

"Naturally! You don't imagine I'm going to charter a helicopter to save you a half-mile walk, do you?

You're not to hang about enjoying yourselves: you're to return to school and watch the senior cricket game until tea-time."

The car turned in through the vicarage gates and the headmaster and his passengers alighted. They were unhitching the trailer as Miss Thorpe came tripping across the lawn to greet them.

"So kind of you, Mr. Oakes," she trilled. "I don't know how we should have managed without these extra chairs."

He smiled politely. "I've brought a couple of young helpers along to set them up for you and—ah—generally make themselves useful," he said, waving a hand in the boys' direction. "Unfortunately, I can't stop—I've an appointment in Dunhambury, but there's no hurry for the chairs or the trailer. I'll arrange to pick them up to-morrow."

For about a quarter of an hour after the headmaster had left, Jennings and Darbishire hurried to and fro in the warm sunshine unpacking the chairs, carrying them across the lawn and setting them up on the far side of the refreshment tent.

By the time the last one was in place both boys were red in the face, bathed in perspiration and sagging at the knees with exhaustion.

Miss Thorpe came along as they were mopping their brows. "My goodness, you have been working hard," she exclaimed in admiration. "And in this heat too. You've certainly earned a glass of lemonade and an ice-cream."

"Thank you," they said, and looked as thirsty as they knew how.

She glanced at her watch. "We shall be serving teas at four o'clock, so if you'd like to have a look round first and then come back to the refreshment tent——"

"We'd love to," Jennings assured her. "And if you could find us any more jobs we'd be ever so pleased, really we would."

There was nothing they could do at the moment she told them, but if they were willing to wait until the maypole dancing was over they could carry the chairs back again and load up the trailer.

"I say, Jen, are you sure it's all right staying on like this?" Darbishire said doubtfully as the boys set off to sample the attractions of the fête. "The Head said we'd got to go straight back to school when we'd done the chairs."

"No, he didn't. He said we'd got to go back as soon as Miss Thorpe didn't need us any more," Jennings corrected. It had already occurred to him that this could be used as a foolproof excuse to cover their absence for as long as they cared to stay. "The Head's gone off to Dunhambury, and Mr. Hind doesn't know what time we're supposed to be back, and Miss Thorpe doesn't know this is supposed to be a punishment," he went on. "If you ask me, we're sitting pretty. We've only got to persuade her to think of a few jobs for us, and we can waltz back to school at what time we like and nobody can say a thing."

Satisfied with this convincing argument, Jennings

led the way back to the lawn to see what entertainment the Linbury church bazaar had to offer.

They were disappointed. There was a hoop-la stand where Darbishire spent five pence and won nothing; and a Lucky Dip where Jennings, to his deep disgust, picked out a small parcel containing a baby's teething ring. There was a stall selling knitted bed-jackets and felt tea-cosies, and another one selling home-grown rhubarb and home-made pickles. There were competitions for estimating the weight of a cake and guessing the name of a hideous plastic doll. But none of these pursuits held much appeal for a couple of boys intent on enjoying a stolen afternoon's freedom.

"This is hopeless. I'd rather be back at school watching the cricket than mooching round here," Darbishire complained after making a tour of the lawns.

"We can't go yet. She's promised us ice-cream and lemonade and we may even get a full-blown tea if we're lucky," Jennings pointed out. He waved his hand towards the far end of the garden. "Let's go and see what they've got down there."

On a patch of rough grass beyond the formal lawns, a small group of people were engaged in the entertaining pastime of *Bowling for a Pig*. The apparatus was simple, consisting of a plank laid lengthways on its side with holes through which the aspiring pig-winner had to roll a number of wooden balls. Above the holes were numbers, running from one to ten; and according to the rules displayed on a poster near-by, the pig would be awarded to the competitor who, at the end of the afternoon, had made the highest score with six consecutive balls.

When the boys arrived the vicar had just scored a miserable five points out of a possible sixty. The local postman who tried next managed a score of no more than seventeen, and he was followed by a young man who turned out to be the captain of the village cricket team. His score was a paltry twenty-one.

"Must be more difficult than it looks," Darbishire surmised.

"No it isn't. They're just rotten shots, that's all," retorted Jennings. "Like you bowling for the Outer Space XI."

Darbishire ignored the insult and said: "Huh! I'd like to see you do better!"

"I could too! What do you bet me I couldn't score as many as that last chap who had a go?"

Darbishire considered. The charge was five pence for six balls. "I won't bet you, but I'll treat you to a free bash if you'll pay me to have another go on the hoop-la."

"Right!" Jennings queued up for his turn and soon found himself with six balls at his feet, facing the target ahead.

His first two shots hit the plank and bounced back without scoring. With his third ball he scored *one*, missed again with his fourth and managed to get his fifth delivery through a hole to score another *three* points.

Darbishire was convulsed with derisive mirth. "Ha!

Look at old Bighead!" he jeered. "Couldn't hit a haystack with a squashed tomato! *Four*—that's all you've scored! I could do better than that blindfold with both hands tied behind my back."

Jennings didn't answer. He seemed to be lost in concentration. Then, he lined up his last ball and sent it shooting through the central arch to score the maximum ten points.

"Fourteen!" said Darbishire. "You're no better than the others. That's what comes of swanking."

But Jennings's success with his last ball had given him new confidence. He turned to his friend with eyes gleaming with inspiration. "I've found out the secret, Darbi! That last ball of mine: it went straight through, didn't it!"

"So what! The others didn't."

"That's the whole point. The ground's so bumpy that you haven't got a chance. But there's one little patch just opposite the middle hole. If you aim for that it's bound to roll through. You can't miss. I didn't discover the secret till I'd only got one ball left."

Darbishire dropped his mocking tone. "Wow! Sounds as though you're on to something. What are you going to do, then?"

"Have another go, of course," Jennings answered excitedly. "It'd be crazy not to, now we've discovered the trick."

Once more he gave his name to the young man in a check shirt and blue jeans who was in charge of the event. Once more he knelt and took aim with the first of the six balls at his feet.

But it still wasn't as easy as he had hoped. He managed to aim his first ball on to the helpful patch of turf, but it failed to run true and bounced back off the plank without scoring. With his second shot he scored *eight* and with the next one *nine*, as the balls veered away slightly to left and right, but still managed to find the archways on either side of the hole that he was aiming at.

The next two balls were frustrating near-misses. Both rolled in a straight line towards the coveted centre arch—and both stopped short just before reaching it.

Jennings was in despair. With five balls he had scored only seventeen points. This was no better than the postman and considerably worse than the captain of the cricket team. And now, to make matters worse, he'd blocked the entrance to the hole he'd been aiming at with his two previous balls.

"Bad luck!" Darbishire observed. "What are you going to do about *that*!"

Jennings shrugged. "Hopeless, isn't it!"

Abandoning all hope of improving his score, the boy hurled the last ball at the plank without taking any aim at all . . . Then came the fluke! The ball struck the nearer of the two balls blocking the hole which, in turn, rolled forward and hit the ball in front.

The result was spectacular: the two balls shot straight forward through the arch followed by the ball that had struck them. Cheers and gasps broke out from the little group of spectators.

"See that! Scored thirty with one ball, he did," the postman informed the vicar.

"Splendid, splendid!" The vicar beamed his congratulations at the youngest competitor. "Well done, young fellow! Very fine effort."

"Just a lucky shot, actually," said Jennings trying to look modest, but quite unable to control the note of triumph in his voice.

The cricket captain turned to the organizer. "How many did he score altogether, then?"

The young man in the check shirt consulted his notebook. "Eight plus nine plus thirty makes forty-seven. Best score so far; but just you wait till old Clive turns up and has a go. He's good for over fifty any day. Can't miss when he's got his eye in, Clive can't."

"That rules you out then, Jen," Darbishire observed with a grimace. "Unless there's a second prize, of course. You might stand a chance of winning that." He turned to consult the poster setting forth the rules of the competition and a broad grin spread over his face. "How about this, then! Second prize is a jar of bath crystals."

"Never use them," Jennings retorted firmly. "Anyway, I wasn't trying to win a prize. I was just showing you I wasn't such a rotten shot as you were trying to make out."

It was now past four o'clock and a loudspeaker was announcing that tea was being served in the refreshment tent. Thirsty and hopeful, the boys made their way over to the marquee trusting that Miss Thorpe would remember her invitation to the hard-working deck-chair attendants.

She did not fail them. Though the tent was crowded with customers she had kept a place for them in the far corner beyond the tea urns, and there they sat eating sandwiches, cakes and ice-cream and drinking lemonade until good manners suggested that they should decline any more.

"Whew! Considering we're supposed to be in detention we're not doing too badly, are we!" Jennings remarked as he finished his third plateful of ice-cream. "Jolly sight better than going on a mouldy picnic with old Wilkie."

Darbishire was still inclined to be worried about the liberties they were taking with the headmaster's instructions. "I suppose it's still all right staying out like this," he demurred. "We've been here an hour already."

"So what! We're doing exactly what the Head told us to—helping Miss Thorpe. We'll push off round about half past five and get back to school in nice time for another tea at six o'clock."

They didn't watch the maypole dancing. Instead, they lost another five pence at the hoop-la stall and spent some time watching a group of burly farm-workers trying to toss a bale of straw over a pole suspended like a rugger goal-post fifteen feet above the ground. And when the dancing was over they carried the deck-chairs back across the garden and stacked them on the trailer.

By now the fête was drawing to a close. One after another the stall-holders packed up their wares as customers wandered away and business dropped to a standstill. The loudspeaker announced the winners of the cake-guessing, doll-naming and pig-bowling competitions, but the quality of the sound was so distorted that nobody could make out a word.

"We'd better say good-bye to Miss Thorpe and then we'll beat it," Jennings decided. "We don't want to hang about too long in case we get nabbed to help with the washing-up, or something."

They were crossing the lawn on their way to the refreshment tent when they were hailed by a shout from behind. Turning, they saw the young man in the check shirt and blue jeans hastening towards them.

"Hey! Your name's Jennings, isn't it?" he demanded as he caught them up.

The boy admitted his identity with a nod. "Yes, that's me. Why?"

"Didn't you hear the loudspeaker asking for you?"

"I heard it going blah-blah-blah, but I couldn't understand what it said." All of a sudden Jennings felt nervous. If they were sending out messages for him it could only mean that the headmaster had returned unexpectedly to take them back to school. They had their excuse for staying on, of course; but it wasn't such a good excuse that Mr. Pemberton-Oakes couldn't demolish it with a few awkward questions if he had a mind to do so.

Uneasily, Jennings turned to his informant and asked: "Do you happen to know what I'm wanted for?"

The young man in the check shirt nodded affably and produced his notebook.

"Top score forty-seven . . . You've won the pig," he said.

CHAPTER 6

# *Pig in a Poke*

JENNINGS WAS so astounded that he rocked on his heels, his eyes opened wide and his jaw dropped.

"Won the pig! But I can't have!" he cried in alarm. "I didn't even *mean* to win it. I wasn't even *trying*!"

There was, indeed, every good reason for his shocked surprise, for his motive in entering for the competition had been solely to impress Darbishire with his skill at bowling a straighter ball than the vicar, the postman or the captain of the local cricket team. His achievement had been a reward in itself and he had given no thought to what might happen afterwards.

Now, for the first time, he was facing the fact that the pig was a real, live creature needing food and shelter and that he—J. C. T. Jennings—was being held responsible for its welfare.

"This is crazy! You'll have to get somebody else to take it," he protested.

The young man in blue jeans looked puzzled. It was rare in his experience for a prize-winner to make such a fuss about the fruits of his victory.

"It's all yours now, chum. Nothing to do with me,"

he replied. "You shouldn't have had a go if you didn't want to win it."

"I didn't think. Besides, you said somebody else would win. I heard you."

"That's right," Darbishire confirmed, rallying to his friend's support. "That chap who always scores fifty. Never misses when he's got his eye in, you told us."

"You mean old Clive?"

"That's the one. 'Just wait till he turns up,' you said. Why didn't *he* win it?"

"Never turned up."

Jennings flipped his fingers in exasperation. "What about the chap who came second, then? I'll swop my pig for his bath-salts."

The young man shook his head. "Too late, chum. He went off on his motor-bike ten minutes ago. He'll be half-way to East Brinkington by now."

The situation was grave. On all sides people were drifting out of the vicarage garden on their way home—happy, carefree people untroubled by superfluous pigs, frustrating school rules and unsympathetic headmasters. Jennings turned to the young man in despair. "Will *you* take it, then? You can have it as a present, free of charge," he urged.

"Are you joking!" The young man grinned. "I live in a council flat, over Dunhambury way. We can't keep a canary in our block without the neighbours creating. I can just imagine what they'd say if I set up a pig-unit on the top-floor landing." He gave Jennings a reassuring pat on the shoulder. "Don't look so worried, chum. You'll find a good home for it in the next day or so. I'll go and get it for you now. My bus goes in ten minutes."

He moved away to the far end of the garden where, until now, the coveted prize had been spending the afternoon in a shady pen behind the rhododendrons.

The boys stared after him in wide-eyed dismay. "All very well saying we'll find a home in a day or so," Jennings said bitterly. "We've got to find a home for it right *now*, before we can go back to school."

Darbishire pursed his lips and said doubtfully. "I suppose we couldn't take it back with us, just for the time being? After all, there's no actual school rule about not having a porker on the premises, is there?"

Jennings snorted. "You need your head seeing to! If it comes to that, there's no actual school rule about not keeping a shoal of jellyfish in the swimming-bath, but you wouldn't be very popular if you tried. Besides," he went on, pressing home the full horror of their dilemma, "besides, this is ten times worse than just turning up at school with *any* old pig that somebody's given us. What you don't seem to realize is that we should never have won the wretched thing if we hadn't been disobeying the Head's orders."

They fell silent, wondering what excuse they could offer. The headmaster had certainly said that they were to help Miss Thorpe while she had need of them: but he had also forbidden them to take part in the afternoon's entertainment. It would be difficult to make him see that bowling for a pig formed part of their duties in setting out the deck-chairs.

Just then, Miss Thorpe emerged from the tea tent. "Just going, are you?" she chirruped, beaming with goodwill. "Mind you tell Mr. Oakes what useful boys you've been when you get back."

"We'll tell him," Jennings assured her. "But the trouble is we can't actually *go* back to school just at the moment because—er—well because something awkward has happened."

She listened sympathetically while he told her about the pig. Even though she was unaware of the headmaster's instructions, she was willing to agree that a well-regulated boarding school might not have the proper facilities for looking after odd items of livestock. She had no idea who had given the pig to the fête committee, she told them; and in any case it would be ungracious to return it to the donor for fear he should think his generous gift was being spurned.

"We'll have to think of some other home for it," she decided. "There must be plenty of people who—" She broke off, her eyes lighting up with inspiration. "Why, of course! Mr. Arrowsmith over at Kettlebridge Farm. He's got a pig-unit. I expect he'll be only too pleased to take in another little guest if you ask him nicely."

The boys knew the farm well, for the footpath leading from the school grounds to Linbury village ran across the fields and meadows owned by Mr. Arrowsmith. The farmer himself they knew less well, although—like all the other boys in the school—they were on polite, cap-raising terms whenever they chanced to meet him.

Jennings and Darbishire were delighted with Miss Thorpe's suggestion. Here, it seemed, was the obvious way out of their troubles.

"Put him in the back of my car, Ronnie," Miss Thorpe commanded when the young man in blue jeans reappeared carrying a surprisingly small but active bundle wrapped in a sack. She turned to the boys. "You can come with me and explain to Mr. Arrowsmith. I'm sure he'll be willing to help."

Miss Thorpe's vehicle was an estate car, so old and shabby in appearance that a small pig in the luggage compartment did not look at all out of place. The boys sat in front of the pig, and Miss Thorpe sat in front of the boys. Narrowly missing the headmaster's trailer, she steered the car out through the vicarage gates and along the road to Kettlebridge Farm.

They were there in five minutes. No one was about as the car made its way past the milking-parlour and came to rest at the entrance to the pig-unit a hundred yards farther on.

"We'll find somewhere to put him and then you can go up to the house and explain," Miss Thorpe said as they all got out of the car.

Darbishire looked worried. "Won't you come with us to ask?" he urged. "It might sound better coming from a grown-up."

She trilled with laughter. "Nonsense! Mr. Arrowsmith won't eat you. In any case, I can't stop. I've got to get back to the vicarage to see to the clearing-up."

Grunts, snorts and squeals disturbed the peace of the late afternoon as they stood looking for a temporary resting-place for the passenger in the luggage compartment. On their right was the farrowing-house, and on their left a row of brick-built pig-sties, each consisting of an inner compartment at the rear with an outdoor concrete forecourt fenced round with iron railings.

Most of the pens were occupied: sows were snoozing in their front gardens with piglets running in and out of the living-rooms.

"Better not dump him in with any of this lot. We don't want a fight on our hands," Jennings observed as they made their way past the squealing litters. But at the end of the row they came across a sty with an unoccupied run and no sign of life within which appeared ideal for their purpose.

"How about this! We'll bung him in here for now," Jennings decided, and Miss Thorpe went back to drive the car alongside to make things easier for the pig-handlers.

In point of fact, the sty was not empty in spite of its deserted appearance. Asleep in the rear compartment was Kettlebridge Susannah the Eighth, the finest Landrace sow that Mr. Arrowsmith had ever reared in all his years as a pig-breeder. Susannah was a majestic animal with all the finer points of her breed developed to perfection. In two weeks' time she would be on display at the County Agricultural Show, and her proud owner had no doubt that she would not only win first prize in her class, but would also have the distinction of being hailed as champion sow of East Sussex.

But at the moment Susannah the Eighth, pride of the Kettlebridge herd, was snoring softly in the straw, unaware that plans were afoot to invade the privacy of her sty.

Jennings opened the rear door of the car and, assisted by Darbishire, lifted the wriggling sack out of the back and laid it down gently on the six-foot square of concrete beyond the railings. After that, he untied the string and eased the little animal out.

Then, for the first time, he was able to take a proper look at the prize he had so thoughtlessly won. Darbishire looked too, and so did Miss Thorpe: whereupon all three of them winced, drew a deep breath and shook their heads sadly at the sight that met their eyes.

In most litters there is always one piglet who fails to come up to expectations—a specimen so weak and so weedy, so uncouth and so ugly that any self-respecting farmer is only too glad to get rid of it.

Jennings's prize was a perfect example of the pig that nobody could be proud of. It was puny in stature and repulsive in aspect: its hind legs were bandy and its fore legs were knock-kneed; its ears drooped, its back was arched and its tail hung straight down behind like a bit of old rope; its eyes were dull and its skin was a size too large for its body. It was, without doubt, the most pathetic-looking specimen of livestock that ever tottered about on four spindly legs.

"H'm! *He'll* never win a prize at the cattle show," said Miss Thorpe.

For a few moments the little pig stood where Jennings had placed it, looking round in a vague and listless manner. Then, alarmed at finding itself in new surroundings, it bolted in through the entrance of the inner compartment and huddled down in the straw in a dark corner.

No sound came from within. Kettlebridge Susannah the Eighth slept on undisturbed by the snufflings of her humble lodger.

"That's that, then! I'll be getting back to the vicarage." Miss Thorpe swung open the door of the car. "It'll be safe enough in there while you go and find Mr. Arrowsmith."

"We'll do that right away," Jennings assured her. "And thank you ever so much for helping us."

The car reversed past the pig-sties and disappeared round the corner of the farrowing-house. Jennings and Darbishire trotted off in the opposite direction heading for the farmhouse which lay on a stretch of rising ground some distance away to their right.

They had gone about two hundred yards when Darbishire said: "I hope he's in. We jolly well *must* get back to school before old Wilkie and the picnic chaps, or we'll be properly up the spout."

"We'll manage all right; don't panic." With the end of his troubles in sight, Jennings was feeling light-hearted again. "I've rather enjoyed myself this afternoon—apart from winning the pig, of course," he admitted. "In fact, I'd say that not being allowed to go on the picnic is one of the decentest punishments I've had for a long time."

They had reached the gate of the farmhouse by now, and Jennings happened to glance back over his shoulder at the outbuildings they had just left at the foot of the slope. "Hey, there's Mr. Arrowsmith down by the piggery," he exclaimed. "We're wasting time going up to see if he's in."

Darbishire followed the direction of his friend's pointing finger. Two burly figures could be seen rounding the corner of the farrowing-house. "Yes, that's Mr. Arrowsmith," he agreed. "But who's that chap he's talking to? Must be a stranger. I've never seen him round these parts before."

Jennings shrugged. "So what! Mr. Arrowsmith doesn't have to ask your permission before he shows somebody round his own property, does he?" He turned and started to retrace his steps down the path. "Come on, Darbi, let's catch them up before they go beetling off out of sight, somewhere."

There was really no mystery about the identity of the tall stranger in the light tweed suit who was being shown round the farm by his host: Tom Weston, like his friend Jim Arrowsmith, was a farmer and breeder of Landrace pigs. He lived a few miles from Linbury and had driven over that afternoon to have a look at Kettlebridge Susannah the Eighth and to give his opinion on the sow's chances in the County Show. The two men had been inspecting some new machinery in the milking-parlour when Miss Thorpe and the boys arrived, and they had no idea that anything unusual had occurred. Now, as they came out into the yard and made their way along to the pig-unit, Mr. Arrowsmith was beaming with anticipation. He had left the big treat of the afternoon until last.

"Come and have a look at her, Tom," he said, hurrying his friend past the sties full of squealing piglets. "She's a real beauty. I've looked after that sow as though she was my own daughter."

"Have you, now!" As a keen but friendly rival in the Landrace competition, Mr. Weston was not going to be too lavish in his praise. "You think she's got a chance of winning, then?"

"A *chance* of winning!" Mr. Arrowsmith was shocked by his friend's patronizing tone. "You don't know what you're talking about, Tom. She's *bound* to win. She's the finest sow that's been bred around these parts for years. Just you wait till you see her!"

With these confident words Jim Arrowsmith led the way forward to the last sty in the row. The outer compartment was empty as they approached, and the farmer winked at his friend and gave him a playful nudge in the ribs.

"This'll be an eye-opener for you, Tom. I'll bet you've never seen a sow like this before in all your born days." So saying, the proud owner called aloud: "Come on then, Susannah! Come on then, old girl!"

There was a rustling of straw in the sleeping quarters and a four-legged object appeared in the forecourt. The object was a pig, or rather a grotesque parody of a pig—a dwarfish, ugly creature with arched back, bow legs, knock knees, straight tail, watery eyes and grey skin.

It advanced a few paces and coughed quietly, as though fearful of disturbing Kettlebridge Susannah the Eighth still sleeping peacefully in the small back room.

Mr. Arrowsmith nearly had a heart attack.

"What's this, eh! What's this!" he roared. He turned to see his friend doubled-up with mirth, tears streaming down his face and clutching the wall of the sty for support.

"Ha-ha-ha! So this is the famous sow, eh, Jim!"he gasped between bellows of laughter. "You'll win first prize with this one, all right! First prize in the camel-backed, spaniel-eared, rat-tailed, Landrace-crossed-armadillo class." He dabbed his streaming eyes. "It was a good joke, Jim. Took me in properly, you did!"

Outraged, Mr. Arrowsmith rounded on his friend. "Joke! What d'you mean, *joke*?"

"Pulling my leg about your breeding a champion and bringing me five miles to have a look at it."

"But I *have* got a champion! Finest sow in the county; and when I lay my hands on the joker who dumped this—this monstrosity in Susannah's pen I'll—I'll . . ."

He broke off as two boys in school caps came running along the path towards him. The taller of the two, hurrying ahead of his companion, skidded to a halt beside the pig-sty and looked up at the irate farmer with a disarming smile.

"Good afternoon, Mr. Arrowsmith," he said politely. "We've got some good news for you. . . . We've brought you a nice little pig to add to your collection."

* * * *

For the second time in less than half a minute Mr. Arrowsmith fought to gain control of his feelings.

"Did *you* do this?" he shouted. "Did you put this repulsive beast in with my prize sow?"

The boys looked surprised. "We thought the sty was empty," Jennings defended himself.

"Oh, you did, did you! Well, you thought wrong."

As though in confirmation of this statement, a second animal appeared in the entrance to the small back room—a superb Landrace with a straight back, bright eyes, curly tail and ears well forward: Kettlebridge Susannah the Eighth, awakened by her master's voice, was emerging to see what all the fuss was about.

Tom Weston whistled in admiration when he saw her. "Whew! You've got a winner there all right, Jim. Finest beast I've set eyes on for years!"

But this was no moment to appraise the sow's unique qualities, for just then Susannah caught sight of the intruder snuffling round her feeding-trough.

She rushed forward to attack and Mr. Arrowsmith,

with a cry of alarm, leaped into the sty and grabbed the little pig by the back legs and whisked it away out of reach.

"Oh, well done, Mr. Arrowsmith! That was brave of you," Darbishire said as the farmer climbed back over the wall holding the wriggling animal firmly by its legs. "That beefy, great brute would just about have made mincemeat of the little one, if you hadn't rescued it."

Jim Arrowsmith snorted in disgust. "I couldn't care less what happens to this ugly little runt. It's Susannah I'm worried about. Supposing she'd scratched herself!" He shuddered at the thought of his prize sow's narrow escape. "What mischief are you boys up to? How dare you play practical jokes on me!" he stormed.

"It wasn't a joke, honestly. You see I won this pig at the Linbury church fête and we were hoping——"

"*Where* did you say you won it?" Tom Weston asked.

"The church fête. I bowled for it. Why?"

"Nothing, nothing. I only wondered." The man turned away with a faintly amused smile and appeared to be admiring the scenery.

But Mr. Arrowsmith was *not* amused. Neither was he smiling. "Disgraceful behaviour! Upsetting my sow, ruining her chances and risking her health with this horrible thing breathing germs all over the feeding-trough." He thrust the small pig into Jennings's arms. "Take it away, at once. I'm not having it in contact with my pigs at any price."

"Oh, but, Mr. Arrowsmith——"

"At once, d'you hear! Get it out of my sight before I——" The words trailed away in speechless fury.

Jennings would have wrung his hands in despair if only his arms had been free of wriggling pig. "But I *can't* take it away. I can't even carry it. It won't keep still!"

Just then, a tractor with a trailer in tow rumbled past the end of the pig-unit heading for the farm gates. Mr. Arrowsmith hailed the driver, telling him to draw alongside.

"I've got a job for you," he said to the farmhand at the wheel. "Take these two lads—and their wretched pig—up to the school and leave them there."

"But we're not allowed to keep pigs at school," Darbishire cried in dismay. "What on earth are we going to say to the Head!"

"That's your problem! You should have thought that one out before! I've had enough of you two and your pig for one afternoon."

Mr. Arrowsmith swung the pig on to the empty trailer and helped the boys to clamber on afterwards. Then he signalled to the driver to move off and stood watching as the unhappy passengers and their pathetic porker bumped and jogged their way towards the farm gates.

When they had gone Jim Arrowsmith turned to his friend. "Now we can have a proper look at Susannah. Tut! The cheek of it! Dumping that measly thing in her pen."

Mr. Weston stroked his chin thoughtfully. "Funny

about the pig," he remarked. "As soon as that lad said where he'd got it from, I guessed it must have been one of mine."

"Yours!"

"Yes. Somebody on the church fête committee rang up and asked if I'd let them have a pig for a prize. Well, I wasn't going to give them one that was any good, so I told my stockman to pick out a dud and send it over to Linbury."

Mr. Arrowsmith raised a surprised eyebrow. "Why didn't you say so, then? Why didn't you take it back when they said they didn't want it?"

A slow smile creased the corners of Tom Weston's mouth. "What do you take me for! When a miserable little runt like that turns up in a litter the best thing to do is to get rid of it, with no questions asked." He turned again towards the sty. "Now, Jim, about this sow of yours . . ."

CHAPTER 7

# *Pig-in-the-Middle*

THE PICNIC PARTY arrived back at half past six. Hot, tired and cheerful, they alighted from the bus at the rear entrance to the school grounds and straggled up the dusty track, past the pond at the far edge of the playing-field.

Venables, Temple and Atkinson were at the tail of the procession some way behind their colleagues, when a tractor drawing an empty trailer came down the track towards them on its way to the gate.

"One of Arrowsmith's," Temple observed as the vehicle rumbled past in a swirl of dust. "What's he doing, going down the back way choking everybody to death! They always use the front drive when they come for the pig-swill."

"He hadn't come for the pig-swill. He was going back empty," said Atkinson. "Anyway, it's no business of yours which gate he uses. It's a free country."

They thought no more of the incident until they reached a cluster of greenhouses and outbuildings near the headmaster's garden where the main path led straight on to the school and a narrow lane branched away from it in the direction of the kitchen garden.

Here they found Darbishire crouching down and peering out from behind a rainwater butt. He rose and left his hiding-place as the boys drew level.

"Thank goodness it's only you," he greeted them. "I had to take cover when Mr. Carter and old Wilkie went past, but I reckon it's safe to come out now."

"Why? What's going on? I thought you were supposed to be in detention," said Venables.

Darbishire patted his nose with his finger to imply secrecy. "I'm on guard. I'm the security man. I'm waiting here to tip old Jennings the wink in case any masters come beetling along. He's gone off to the kitchen yard for a barrow-load of pig-swill."

Naturally, they demanded to know what was afoot, so Darbishire recounted the misadventures of the afternoon.

"We asked the chap with the trailer to come in the back way so we wouldn't meet anybody," he finished up. "He was jolly decent, too. He put the pig in the potting-shed for us and told us what to give it to eat."

"You can't leave it in the potting-shed for ever," Atkinson pointed out.

"We know that. We haven't worked out what we're going to do yet."

"Yes, but what's the Head going to say when he finds out you've . . ." Atkinson broke off as Jennings came round the corner from the kitchen yard trundling a wheelbarrow containing cabbage leaves, bread crusts, potato peel and the remains of seventy-nine bowls of porridge served up that morning for school breakfast.

The security man beckoned him on. "All clear!" he reported, and turned to the others. "If you lot want to be useful you can help guard the door while Jen takes the food in. We don't want him escaping and running amok."

The wheelbarrow clanked to a stop outside the potting-shed. Venables, Temple and Atkinson crouched before the entrance with hands extended like fielders in the slips while Darbishire opened the door just wide enough to allow Jennings and the barrow to squeeze through.

"He's eating it," the amateur pigman announced when he came out a few minutes later. "Making a real hog of himself." He went into a nearby greenhouse and emerged with a bucket which he filled from the water butt. Again the potting-shed door was edged open and the drinking water was pushed inside.

"Come on! Time we weren't here—or some master will start creating." Jennings turned and led the way up the track to the quad where Mr. Hind was on supervision duty. He beckoned to Jennings and Darbishire as they approached and waved the other three boys on.

"Where have you two been?" the master demanded. "I understood from the Head that you would be coming over to watch the senior cricket when he'd finished with you."

Mr. Hind was a tall, pale young man with a drawling voice who taught art and music. Out of school hours he invariably had a short cherry-wood pipe clenched between his teeth, and his whereabouts could usually be traced by following the trail of tobacco smoke which floated behind him like a thin, grey ghost.

Jennings thought fast. Mr. Hind did not seem unduly concerned about their long absence, so it was possible that he had been given only a rough idea of the headmaster's intentions.

"Well you see sir, the Head took us to the fête to put the chairs out and to help Miss Thorpe," he explained. "And what with one thing and another we—sort of—got delayed."

"Did you, indeed!"

"Yes sir, but we're back now so—er—so——" Jennings broke off, thinking about the pig in the potting-shed. "Do you happen to know whether the Head's back too, sir? There's something I *may* have to see him about."

"You can't see him to-night. He won't be back till after you're in bed," Mr. Hind told him. He pointed towards the dining-hall with the stem of his pipe. "Off you go! It's time for milk and biscuits."

So far as Mr. Hind was concerned, the boys had managed to steer clear of trouble: but this was cold comfort when they thought of the more serious problems still to be faced.

What on earth was to be done about the pig? In the dormitory that evening Jennings and Darbishire discussed their dilemma with their friends in the hope of finding a way out. But there *was* no way out, and finally everybody had to agree that the only thing to do was for the culprits to go and see Mr. Pemberton-Oakes as soon as possible and own up.

"Try and break it to him gently so he doesn't go off like an H-bomb," Venables advised. "It's no good saying: 'Please, sir, there's a porker in the potting-shed because we defied your commands!' Be tactful and wrap it up in a lot of old flannel about wanting to be kind to dumb animals and all that."

"Couldn't we put it off till next week some time?" Darbishire said in worried tones. "We might be able to find somebody to take him off our hands if we think hard for a day or two."

Temple shook his head. "Too risky! You've got to feed him twice a day and somebody would be bound to see you or Jen rummaging through the pig bins, and then what could you say?"

"They could say they were hungry," said Atkinson. He could afford to make facetious suggestions as he, personally, was not involved. In more serious vein he went on: "The longer you put it off, the more chance there is of the Head going to the potting-shed to get a trowel or something."

Jennings nodded in agreement. Better to own up freely than to be found out afterwards. "We'll go and tell him to-morrow, Darbi. First thing after breakfast," he decided.

The following day was Sunday: and in the cool, clear light of morning the idea of confronting Mr. Pemberton-Oakes seemed even less attractive than it had done the night before.

Perhaps after chapel would be a better time, Jennings thought, as he sat at the breakfast-table toying with his hard-boiled egg. Perhaps the headmaster would be in a more charitable frame of mind after singing hymns about mercy and forgiveness.

But the delay was fatal. After the service, Mr. Pemberton-Oakes left by one door while the boys were sent out by another. Mr. Wilkins who was on duty wouldn't listen to Jennings's plea, and sent him straight off to his classroom to write his weekly letter to his parents.

After letter-writing, it was time for lunch; and it was not until the meal was over and the arrangements for the afternoon had been announced, that Jennings and Darbishire had a chance to slip away to the headmaster's study.

As it happened, the programme for the afternoon had some bearing on the events which followed, so it would not, perhaps, be out of place to summarise the arrangements.

Normally, the school went for walks on Sunday afternoons, but towards the middle of the summer term when the weather was too hot for vigorous exercise, the formal Sunday walk was cancelled. Instead, the whole school went out on to the playing-field with books, stamp albums, puzzles or indoor games and spent an hour or so occupying themselves in quiet and peaceful recreation.

This, then, was the order of the day; and at half past two, the boys made their way out of doors to read their books or pursue their hobbies on the shady side of the games field.

Venables took a library book, Bromwich took his camera, and Temple and Martin-Jones had a writing-pad on which to play an outdoor game of indoor cricket. Rumbelow and Atkinson carried a chess board and chessmen, and Binns and Blotwell, the youngest boys in the school, a jigsaw puzzle of five hundred pieces, depicting knights in armour storming a medieval castle, which they had been patiently putting together since the first day of term.

So far, they had assembled four hundred and fifty-six of the pieces and were hoping to complete the puzzle by the end of the day. They walked with extreme care, fearful lest some clumsy movement or chance collision should jog the large square of hardboard on which the results of their labours to date were laid out with painstaking precision.

By a quarter to three, seventy-seven of the seventy-nine boarders of Linbury Court School had spread themselves around the games field and were engaged in interesting or instructive occupations. The two remaining boarders—listed on the register as Jennings, J. C. T. and Darbishire, C. E. J.—were standing outside the headmaster's study awaiting an answer to the hesitant knock which Jennings had just delivered on the door.

There was no answer to Jennings's knock. Five minutes earlier, Mr. Pemberton-Oakes had wandered out into his garden to enjoy the sunshine and admire his roses. The weather was so warm that he decided to spend the rest of the afternoon reading in a deck-chair, but before doing so he thought he would stroll as far as the playing-field to see how the boys were enjoying the new Sunday afternoon routine.

As he was passing the potting-shed he heard a scuffling noise coming from within. Surely, it couldn't be a rat! Perhaps some boy was breaking bounds and up to mischief!

Sternly, the headmaster called: "Who's that in there? Come out, at once, that boy in the potting-shed!"

There was no answer and the scuffling noise continued. Puzzled, Mr. Pemberton-Oakes strode up to the shed, lifted the latch and flung the door open wide. As he did so a small, four-legged object came catapulting out, shot through his legs and bolted off as fast as it could go.

The headmaster stared after it in amazement. What on earth was a pig doing on the premises? It must be rounded up at once before it could do any damage! He hurried after it at a dignified trot.

So far as doing any damage was concerned, the pig had already started on a trail of destruction. First it ran into the headmaster's garden, charging across the flower beds, uprooting shrubs and sending plants flying in all directions.

Then it broke through the hedge and scuttled away to the playing-field where the first thing it encountered was the five hundred-piece jigsaw puzzle.

Startled, Binns and Blotwell leaped to their feet as the pig ran between them, skidding over the hardboard and scattering the four hundred and fifty-six assembled pieces like chaff from a harvester.

Two seconds later it darted beneath the folding canvas chair in which Mr. Wilkins was sitting, upsetting the supports and depositing the master flat on his back.

All round the field, boys jumped to their feet and chased after the little creature in the hope of effecting a capture.

They hoped in vain. A human being on two legs has little chance against a lively animal on four; and the pig, though puny, was surprisingly agile. Back and forth round the games field it ran with the boys in pursuit. Three times it seemed on the point of being cornered, and three times it escaped with a wriggle and a rush from the unskilled hands of its captors.

"This is ridiculous," the headmaster complained to Mr. Wilkins as they stood watching the scene of commotion. By now the pig had reached the cricket square where its hoofs were churning up large divots of the sacred turf every time it changed direction. "Just look at the damage it's doing to the First XI pitch! If we don't catch it soon, we'll have to cancel our matches for the rest of the term."

Just then Mr. Carter arrived, having heard the sounds of the chase from the staff-room window. He sized up the situation at a glance. "The first thing to do is to call the boys off," he said. "They're doing more harm than good, chasing after it like that. It's so frightened it doesn't know what it's doing."

"What do you suggest, then?" the headmaster asked.

Mr. Carter took charge. First, he ordered all the boys to retire to the edge of the field, and then to form up again in a circle with the pig in the middle. At a point on the circumference was a cricket net, and it was Mr. Carter's plan for the trappers gradually to reduce the size of the circle and so head the little animal into the net. He stationed a boy on each of the guy-ropes supporting the net poles with orders to slacken the lines at a given signal. Then, in silence and without fuss, the round-up began.

The little pig, still frisky, but no longer in a blind panic, tended to run forward as the circle closed in. After several false starts and narrow escapes it was driven by degrees across the turf to the very edge of the trap. Here it stopped for nearly half a minute. Then, to the onlookers' dismay, it turned and started to run out again.

It was a moment of crisis. If the pig escaped through the ring of trappers, the plan would have failed. Seeing the danger, Mr. Wilkins broke out of the circle and charged forward at full speed driving the animal before him back into the net. As pursued and pursuer rushed headlong towards the rear of the trap, Mr. Carter shouted: "Let go!"

The boys on the guy-ropes released their hold, the supporting poles fell forward and a thousand square feet of cricket netting dropped down to enmesh the quarry in its folds.

The circle of trappers raised a cheer—then looked again and saw that they had secured not one captive, but *two*! . . . Parcelled up near the open end like shopping in a string bag was Mr. Wilkins, who had been unable to stem his forward rush before the net collapsed on top of him.

For a while the master floundered around like a competitor in an obstacle race; then on hands and knees he groped his way to the edge of the net, and scrambled through to freedom.

At the other end of the net the pig, who had been struggling as strenuously as Mr. Wilkins, gave up and allowed Mr. Carter to disentangle it from the folds.

"Where do you want me to put it?" Mr. Carter asked the headmaster, holding the animal securely by its hind legs and its ears.

"Back in the potting-shed, for now—until I've discovered where it belongs. I'd better come with you and lend a hand. We've had enough accidents for one afternoon."

The two masters went off with the pig, leaving the boys to settle once more to their occupations. Soon all was quiet again on the games field—except for the lamentations of Binns and Blotwell faced with the task of finding five hundred tiny pieces of fret-sawn plywood, many of which had come to rest in a bed of nettles.

"I can't think how on earth the wretched animal

managed to shut itself in," the headmaster observed when the captive had been returned to its quarters and the door firmly barricaded. "I'd better ring the police straight away and see if anyone has reported losing it."

"It didn't get in there by chance," Mr. Carter said as they crossed the garden on their way back to the house. "Judging by the remains of cabbage leaves and stale bread crusts on the floor, it's obvious that somebody is in charge of the catering arrangements."

"You think somebody in the school is responsible? Who on earth would want to do a thing like that?"

Mr. Carter smiled and said: "I expect we'll find out before the day's much older."

In the corridor outside the headmaster's study, Jennings and Darbishire were waiting. They had been waiting a long time, but were afraid to go away in case they missed their chance of seeing Mr. Pemberton-Oakes on his return. For more than half an hour they had been cooling their heels in the corridor, quite unaware of the stirring scenes of chaos and capture that had been taking place on the playing-field outside.

Now, they sprang to attention as the masters approached and Jennings said: "Sir, please, sir. Could we see you for a minute, please sir? It's terribly urgent. There's something we've got to tell you."

The headmaster nodded. "What is it?"

"Well, sir, it's not very easy to explain," Jennings went on in hesitant tones. Now that the time for confession had arrived, he was finding Venables's advice to "wrap it up in a lot of old flannel" difficult to put into practice. "You see, sir, it's like this, as you might say. Or rather, in other words—so to speak—to put it another way——" He floundered to a stop. The right words wouldn't come.

"You're not making yourself very clear," the headmaster said. He exchanged a knowing glance with Mr. Carter. "Correct me if I'm wrong, Jennings, but are you trying to tell me that there's a pig in the potting-shed?"

"Yes sir, that's quite right, but—but——" the boy stared up at him in amazement. "However did you guess what I was trying to tell you?"

CHAPTER 8

# *Security Risk*

THE HEADMASTER raised despairing eyes to the ceiling. "You were quite right, Carter. It didn't take us long to find out." He glanced down again at the self-confessed culprits fidgeting uncomfortably before him. "I might have known that these two boys—Jennings, in particular—could be expected to shed some light on the mystery."

Mr. Pemberton-Oakes was a liberal-minded man who prided himself on holding enlightened ideas about education. All the same, he was shocked. Even the most permissive of headmasters resents having his rose trees uprooted, his routine upset and his cricket square looking as though it had been weeded with a road drill.

He led the way into the study followed by Mr. Carter and the fidgeting culprits. Then he began the inquiry.

The facts were soon told and justice—tempered with mercy—meted out. It was not so much the original act of disobedience that raised the headmaster's anger, but rather that a trail of chaos and destruction had followed in its wake.

Accordingly, as part of their punishment, the boys

would have to forfeit their evening recreation for two weeks and to spend the time in re-planting such of the uprooted shrubs as were worth saving. In addition, their morning breaks during this period were to be devoted to smoothing out the bumps and hollows on the cricket square with a garden roller.

The next item on the agenda was the disposal of the livestock.

"You boys can go. I hardly think Mr. Carter and I need your assistance in deciding what's to be done." Mr. Pemberton-Oakes motioned the boys to leave the room and turned to his assistant. "I think I'll give Arrowsmith a ring. I've no doubt he'll be willing to take the animal off our hands."

Jennings spun round in the doorway. "Oh, sir, *no* sir! I shouldn't do that, honestly. Not Mr. Arrowsmith, sir."

The headmaster was taken aback. He was not used to having his decisions disputed by eleven-year-old boys in Form 3. Frigidly, he said: "Jennings, I told you to leave the room."

"Yes I know, sir, but I must warn you. It's urgent. You see, there's something you don't know about."

In his confession of the events of the previous afternoon Jennings had not included the embarrassing interlude at Kettlebridge Farm, as it had made no difference to the outcome. Now, he hastened to fill in the details. ". . . and so you see sir, he'd be furious if anybody asked him again," he finished up. "He told us to get it out of his sight at once—or else."

Mr. Pemberton-Oakes disapproved of adverbs being used in this casual manner. "Or else!" he echoed. "What do you mean—'Or else'? *What* else?"

"Nothing else, sir. Just else—*or else.* Full stop."

The headmaster gave it up. "Go away, Jennings," he said irritably.

No sooner had the boys left than the telephone rang. The caller was Miss Thorpe ringing up to congratulate Mr. Pemberton-Oakes on having amongst his pupils such helpful, willing and co-operative boys as the two who had come along to the fête to set out the chairs.

"They were invaluable," she assured him in her bird-like twitter. "So useful! You must be very proud of them. They kept coming back and asking if there was anything more they could do to help."

The headmaster winced and relieved his feelings by drumming his fingers on his leather-topped desk. "They did one thing that was *not* particularly helpful," he said as soon as he could get a word in edgeways. "They came back with a pig."

Miss Thorpe was surprised. "Oh, but surely! We took it to Kettlebridge Farm as a little present for Mr. Arrowsmith."

"So I understand. Unfortunately, the gift was not appreciated."

"Oh dear, what a pity. Still, it's rather a sweet little piggy. I expect you'll all become quite fond of it when you get to know its little ways."

This time the headmaster winced so sharply that the sound was audible at the other end of the line. "Miss

Thorpe," he said, politely but firmly. "I have already got to know its little ways. And with the exception of an earthquake, a thunderbolt or a volcanic eruption, I can think of nothing which, in the space of twenty minutes, could cause so much dislocation to school routine and damage to school property as the creature you so blandly describe as a sweet little piggy."

Mr. Carter looked out of the window to conceal a smile. From where he was sitting he could see Mr. Wilkins assisted by half a dozen boys still struggling to put up the cricket net on the far side of the games field. Poor Wilkins! he thought. It was odd how these upsets always seemed to occur whenever *he* was on duty!

Across the leather-topped desk Mr. Pemberton-Oakes was saying: "Yes, I appreciate that, Miss Thorpe. It was entirely the fault of the boys: I don't hold you responsible. But as secretary of the fête committee which organized the competition, I was wondering whether you could, perhaps, find some other—ah—worthy claimant for this valuable prize?" He listened while she replied at considerable length. Then he replaced the receiver.

"Miss Thorpe is going to try to find another home for it," he reported to Mr. Carter. "It merely remains for us to see that all is ready at our end."

So saying, the headmaster went off in search of the odd-job man whom he found reading the Sunday paper in the little garden behind his cottage. Could Robinson find a sack? the headmaster inquired. A roomy sack without holes, suitable for containing a small pig in the back of a car? Furthermore, would Robinson be available later in the day to provide a meal for the parting guest and speed it on its way?

Robinson thought he could cope with these requests. Although Sunday was normally a day of rest, he was willing, he said, to make a personal sacrifice when duty called.

It was nearly time for the dormitory bell when Miss Thorpe drove up in her car. Mr. Carter went out on to the quad to greet her. "Any luck?" he inquired.

"Rather! Success at last," she trilled like a blackbird in full-throated song. "I found out that the winner of the second prize for the pig-bowling was Mr. P. Nutt of East Brinkington."

"Splendid! And you think this Mr. Peanut will take our pig?"

"Not Mr. *Pea*nut. The name is Nutt—initial *P*: Peter Nutt."

"I beg your pardon."

"Not at all! I've been over to East Brinkington and he was most co-operative. He keeps a few pigs in his back garden you see and, unlike Mr. Arrowsmith who is *so* particular, he doesn't seem to mind what shape they are, so long as they've got four legs."

Ten minutes later Miss Thorpe drove off on her mission with the pig in the back of the car. Mr. Carter went indoors where he met Darbishire going upstairs to bed.

"Any news about the porker, sir?" the boy asked

anxiously. He brightened visibly when Mr. Carter was able to tell him that all was well.

"Oh, thank goodness, sir. I'm ever so glad you've found a good home for him," Darbishire spoke as though a weight had been taken off his mind. "He must have felt so unhappy and unwanted with everybody saying they wouldn't have him at any price." He smiled as he turned to go up the stairs. "Thanks ever so much, sir. Jennings and I can stop worrying now we know he's going to be looked after by somebody who wants him for his own sake, as you might say."

* * * *

During the next two weeks Jennings and Darbishire had very little time to call their own. Morning break was given up to rolling the cricket pitch and evening break to tidying the rose trees. And on the occasions when they did manage to snatch a few moments freedom, they devoted themselves to quiet and harmless occupations guaranteed not to involve them in any trouble with the masters.

Thus it was that they spent some while in re-arranging their stamp albums and discussing ways in which they could improve their collections. As Jennings had already pointed out, the forthcoming issue of postage stamps to mark a century of scientific inventions would offer a real chance of stealing a march on their fellow-philatelists. If they were lucky enough to acquire some specimens which nobody else could get hold of, their collections would be the envy of their colleagues in Form 3.

This, they decided to do.

"We can get them post-marked on the day of issue easily enough by addressing them to ourselves," Darbishire observed in the common room after school on Wednesday morning. "The big snag's going to be getting hold of the stamps to stick on the envelopes."

Jennings nodded, deep in thought. There were two factors to be considered—time and opportunity. It was unlikely that the Linbury General Stores and Post Office would have more than a token supply to dispose of, and these might all be snapped up in the first hour of the day's trading.

"We can't ask a master to get some for us; they're always too busy to go belting off to the village just before morning school," Darbishire went on. "And even if they weren't, they might find a queue a hundred miles long when they got there, and they'd never agree to be late back for class."

Jennings emerged from his trance of deep thought. "We could ask Pettigrew. He goes past the post office every morning on his way to school."

"Wow! Yes, of course. Super idea!" Darbishire agreed.

Pettigrew was a plump, freckled-faced day boy who lived in a house on the Dunhambury road and cycled to school each day. As it happened he was not a stamp-collector, and so he would not be tempted to buy any of the new issue for himself, thereby ruining the monopoly which Jennings and Darbishire were hoping to create.

"We'll have to do a security check on him though," Jennings decided. "If the news gets out, other chaps will start muscling in and the whole thing will just become a racket." He thought for a moment and added: "And another thing—you'd better tear up that page with the details on in your stamp magazine, in case anybody wants to borrow it."

"Yes, I will. You can't be too careful," Darbishire agreed.

Jennings had a word with Pettigrew in the bicycle shed after school as the day boy was getting ready to go home.

"Listen, Petters, will you do Darbi and me a favour?" he began. "We want you to get us some stamps from the post office on Monday week. It's a new issue,—*Scientific Inventions of the Twentieth Century.*"

"I might—if I remember," Pettigrew agreed vaguely.

"Ah, but it's important. It's a secret, too. We're giving the whole operation top security cover so the other chaps don't get to know about it," Jennings explained. "That means you'll have to be screened as a security risk before I ask you whether you're willing to help us."

"It's a bit late for that. You've already asked me," the security risk pointed out.

"Well, you know what I mean," Jennings dismissed the matter with a shrug. "Now, all you'll have to do is to leave home a bit earlier than usual. Say the post office opens at half past eight," he went on, taking this doubtful fact for granted. "If you get there five minutes before, you can be first in the queue and still get to school by quarter to nine."

The request sounded reasonable and Pettigrew agreed, on condition that the money for the transaction was given to him in advance. "I'm not waiting for months while you hang on to the stamps hoping the market price is going up," he insisted as he wheeled his bicycle out of the shed.

Jennings was shocked. "We're not going to *sell* them. We're just planning to buy them and get them franked so everybody else will go round kicking themselves because they didn't think of doing it, too."

* * * *

On Thursday, Jennings found an envelope on his desk when he and Darbishire went into Classroom 3 shortly before morning school. It was addressed in wobbling block capitals to Messrs. Jennings and Darbishire, Esquire. Inside was a note written on a page torn from a school exercise book. It read:

Dear Messrs. Jennings and Darbishire,

I expect you think that just because you are signior to us being in Form 3 you can throw your wait about and get away with it, but you are wrong so Beware!!!

It is all your fault that we lost 73 bits of the

puzzle so the horses have not got any legs and the castle walls are stuck in mid-air and do not come down to the ground.

It was your rotan old pig that did all the damage and we think Darbishire is a rota and Jennings is a bigger one so what are you going to do about it?

With best wishes,

Yours truly,

Binns and Blotwell.

Jennings was mystified, but Darbishire was able to explain.

"Venables told me our pig knocked their jigsaw puzzle for six on Sunday afternoon," he said. "Can't see what they've got to worry about. If we'd nothing worse on our plates than a mouldy old jigsaw with a few bits of horses' legs missing, we'd be laughing."

Jennings glanced up and spotted the authors of the letter hanging about outside the door, anxious to know how their missive had been received. He called them in.

"Are you peers of the realm?" he inquired. "*Lord* Binns and *Lord* Blotwell?"

They denied having any connection with the aristocracy. "No. Why?"

"Because only Lords are supposed to sign letters with just their surnames. Don't they teach you *anything* in Form One!" Jennings's superior tone concealed the fact that he himself had made the discovery only the day before, when corrected by Mr. Carter for making a similar mistake. "Ordinary human beings have to use their first names or their initials, like, say, for instance, Yours truly, Obadiah Binns, or X. Y. Z. Blotwell."

"But my name isn't Obadiah," Binns objected.

"And if my initials were *really* X. Y. Z. what on earth could they stand for?" Blotwell wanted to know.

Jennings ignored the interruptions. "And what's all this about Darbi and me being rotas? You can be *on* a rota when it's your turn to do something, but you can't *be* one."

"Perhaps they mean we rotate—like Rotarians and people," Darbishire suggested.

"You can't read straight. It's meant to be 'rotter' not 'rota'," Binns explained. "And anyway, just because Jennings——"

"*Signior* Jennings, to you, if you please. And *Signior* Darbishire. You actually admit that's the proper thing to call us in your first sentence."

The letter-writers exchanged baffled glances. "Come on Binns, we're wasting our time talking to these chaps," said Blotwell, making for the door. "They're mad. Everybody in Form 3 is mad."

Jennings called him back. "Supposing you hadn't lost all those pieces," he argued. "You'd have finished your puzzle by now, so what would you do next Sunday afternoon, instead?"

Blotwell shrugged. "Nothing, I suppose."

"Well, there you are then!" Jennings's tone was confident. "Old Wilkie always goes up the wall when chaps tell him they've got nothing to do. He'd have made you go round picking up toffee-papers or something weedy, so you ought to be grateful."

"Grateful! But we *still* shan't have anything to do, if we can't finish the jigsaw."

"Yes, you will. You can go on looking for the bits."

There was a flaw in this argument somewhere, Blotwell thought, but he couldn't quite put his finger on it.

Disgruntled, the jigsaw enthusiasts wandered out into the corridor to discuss in private whether or not they were the victims of some sort of confidence trick.

Binns shook his head sadly and said: "Tut! It's always the same. You can't win with people like third-formers."

"*People!* You can't call third-formers *people*—well, not civilized, human beings like you and me," Blotwell retorted, as the bell rang for morning assembly. "Chaps in Form One are all right, of course. Form Two-ers aren't so bad if only they mind their own business, but after that——" He pulled a long face. "—after that the rot sets in. If you ask me, Form Three-ers in general—and Jennings, in particular—are the lowest form of animal life known to the world of science."

CHAPTER 9

# *False Alarm*

THE LAST LESSON on Friday was a free period for Mr. Carter. He spent the time in the staff room making out the teams for the afternoon's cricket games.

As the bell rang for the end of the lesson, the door opened and a pleasant-looking young woman in nurse's uniform came in wheeling a tea trolley.

"You've saved my life, Matron," he greeted her. "I'm in need of a cup of tea."

"I'm not sure that you deserve one," she replied jokingly. "Just sitting in here smoking your pipe while poor Mr. Wilkins is battling with Form 3."

He laughed. "I, too, have my moments with Form 3, don't forget!"

Matron wheeled the trolley to the window and looked out just as an old, battered estate car drove on to the quad and pulled up with a squealing of brakes. "Miss Thorpe's here again," she announced.

Mr. Carter smote his brow in dismay. "Oh, *no*! Don't say she's brought that pig back!"

"It looks a bit small for a pig, but she's brought *something*."

Mr. Carter joined Matron at the window and together they watched as Miss Thorpe got out of her car clutching a short, cylindrical object wrapped in brown paper. She looked round for someone to attend to her needs and then beckoned to Rumbelow who, just released from school, was coming out through the side door on to the quad.

The boy trotted over to the visitor and stood listening and nodding his head politely while she addressed him at some length. The words were inaudible to the observers in the staff room, but they appeared to consist of instructions, for finally she thrust the brown paper parcel into Rumbelow's hands, got back into her car and drove away.

"A little gift for somebody?" Mr. Carter hazarded. "Perhaps it's for you, Matron."

"Are you joking! I can't imagine who'd want to give me a present." She turned to pour out the tea, and Mr. Carter picked up his lists of cricket teams and crossed to the door.

Outside in the corridor a noise like a herd of bison charging to a water-hole announced that the rest of Form 3 were on their way downstairs to get ready for cricket.

Mr. Carter opened the door and stopped the first charging bison that came within his line of vision.

"A little job for you, Venables," he said, handing the boy the lists he had just been compiling. "Pin these up on the changing-room notice-board, straight away."

"Yes, sir, rather, sir."

"And *walk* down to the changing-room. Try to remember that the staircase is not a ski-jump."

"Yes, sir, rather, sir." Venables glanced at the sheets of paper in his hand. "Could I have some drawing-pins to stick them up with, sir? There are never any left on the notice-board when you want them."

Mr. Carter produced four brass drawing-pins from a box on the staff room mantelshelf. "Here you are. One for each sheet and mind you don't lose them."

There was a jostling crowd around the notice-board waiting for the teams to be posted up, when Venables reached the changing-room.

"Gangway! Gangway!" he commanded, pushing his way through. "And stop shoving. How d'you think I can put the sides up with you lot barging me about all over the place!"

The notice-board was fixed rather too high on the wall for the messenger to be able to pin up his lists in comfort. Looking round for something to stand on, he spotted a bench near the window and dragged it along to the notice-board to use as a platform.

He was just climbing upon it to begin his task when a diversion occurred. Rumbelow came into the room, brandishing in the air a short, cylindrical object wrapped in brown paper. He pushed his way up to the bench calling: "Jennings! Jennings! Anyone seen old Jennings!"

Jennings inched his way forward through the crowd. "Here! What do you want me for?"

"I've just seen your friend Miss What's-it: you know—the one who came last Sunday," Rumbelow told him. "She told me to tell you that the chap who came second in your famous pig-bowling lark has handed back his second prize in exchange for your old porker."

"So he jolly well should—that's only fair," Temple chimed in over Rumbelow's shoulder. "A chap shouldn't hang on to two prizes just for coming second, when the champion doesn't get one at all."

"That's just what she said—more or less," Rumbelow agreed. He thrust the parcel at Jennings. "Here you are! Take it—it's all yours."

If only Jennings had remembered what the second prize consisted of, he would have sought out a less public place before opening the parcel. But, by now, he had forgotten (if, indeed, he had ever given any thought to the matter in the first place) and he tore off the wrapping with some degree of excitement.

He remembered, of course, as soon as he saw the bath salts; but by that time it was too late, for everybody else had seen them too.

There is nothing comical about strongly-perfumed bath salts when considered as an aid to hygiene. But to the forty-six juniors jostling round the notice-board there seemed to be something specially diverting in the idea of awarding an inky-fingered pig-bowling champion with a toilet article of such feminine appeal.

There was a guffaw of laughter as Jennings ripped off the paper—a guffaw which swelled to howls of hysteria as the boys around him caught sight of the label on the jar.

*GLAMOUR*, it read: *The new Fresh 'n' Lovely Exotic Bath Crystals. Specially Blended for the Modern Miss.*

"Jennings, the glamour-girl!" they cried in derision. "Jennings, the specially blended modern miss! . . . Miss Jemima Jennings, the fresh 'n' lovely Beauty Queen of Form 3! . . . Vote for Jennings for Miss World!"

They formed a circle and danced round him with mincing steps in a grotesque imitation of a *corps de ballet.* The derisive laughter gave place to girlish squeals when someone snatched the jar and removed the stopper, so that the air became charged with a strong smell of verbena. At this, some of the dancers collapsed in swoons like Victorian maidens suffering from an attack of the vapours: others fanned the air and held their noses.

"Wow! Coo! Poisonous fumes!" they gasped. "Odious odours! . . . Strong pong! . . . *Eau de Jennings's Bath Night!*"

Jennings stood in the middle trying to look as though he didn't mind, and the dancers increased their efforts, hoping to goad him into some form of retaliation.

The noise was deafening. When it was at its height, Mr. Hind walked in to see whether the boys were getting ready for cricket.

"Silence! Si-lence!" he shouted with the full force of his lungs.

The dancers ceased cavorting, the cat-calls broke off in mid-squawk.

"Disgraceful! What on earth do you boys think you're playing at!" he fumed. "Why aren't you all getting changed for cricket?"

"We were just waiting for Venables to put the teams up, sir," said Bromwich, as though this, in itself, was the reason for the tumult.

Venables was still standing on the bench with the drawing-pins in one hand and his lists in the other. He turned round to the notice-board and accidentally dropped the drawing-pins which scattered at his feet and fell on to the floor.

"Sorry, sir," he apologized, jumping down to retrieve them. "Somebody jogged the bench."

He found three of the pins without any trouble, but the fourth seemed to have vanished without trace. "Sorry, sir," he repeated at five-second intervals as he inspected the cracks between the floorboards. "It must have rolled somewhere."

Mr. Hind tapped his foot on the floor with impatience. "Oh, for goodness' sake, boy! It'll be time to draw stumps before we've even started changing, at this rate." He took the lists and pinned up three with the available drawing-pins. The fourth list he read aloud so that the boys concerned would know which team they had been chosen for.

While this was happening, Jennings retrieved his unwanted property. The jar of bath salts had been put down on the bench close to where Venables had been standing: the glass stopper was rolling about on the floor. As soon as Mr. Hind had finished his announcement, the boy scuttled out of the room and hid his embarrassing prize at the bottom of his tuck box until he could decide what to do with it.

It was Darbishire who suggested the obvious answer. "I should give it to Matron," he said, as he and Jennings came in together after cricket. "Women like bath salts. They don't seem to mind going about ponging like a scent factory."

As it happened, Matron couldn't stand the smell of verbena bath salts, but she was much too polite to say so when Jennings came along to the dispensary at bedtime that evening. He was wearing pyjamas and carrying a cylindrical object wrapped in newspaper which he handed to her with a beaming smile.

"For me? Well this is a surprise," she said as she thanked him. "I was saying to Mr. Carter only this afternoon that I couldn't think why anyone should want to give me a present."

"Oh, I didn't actually *want* to give you one, Matron. I didn't buy it specially, or anything." The donor broke off, frowning. It wasn't a very gracious way of putting it, he thought. "What I mean is, all the chaps agree that you're ever so decent, so I thought you might like a present to prove it. It's *Glamour*, you see, Matron. For the Modern Miss, it says."

"That's very kind of you, Jennings." By way of showing her appreciation she removed the stopper and sniffed—and recoiled at the pungent smell which assailed her nose. Forcing a smile, she added: "I haven't got time to try them now: I'm going out to supper. But I must certainly have a bath before I go to bed to-night, mustn't I?"

Jennings returned to his dormitory delighted that he had disposed of his unwelcome prize to such good purpose. Much better than just chucking the jar in the dustbin he thought. Matron was charmed with the gift, he was quite sure about that. But then, so she jolly well should be: it wasn't every day that someone came along giving her expensively perfumed concoctions specially blended for the Modern Miss!

* * * *

The other boys were already in bed when Jennings reached Dormitory 4. By now, the scene in the changing-room was no more than a stale joke but, even so, Temple couldn't resist saying: "Hullo, Jen! Been for your exotic fresh 'n' lovely splash in the bath-tub?"

Jennings grinned. "Are you kidding! I never use the stuff," he said with a grimace as he jumped into bed. "Actually, I've got rid of it."

From across the room Venables sat up and said: "Just as well, really. That bottle's dangerous. It's got a drawing-pin in it."

Jennings looked puzzled. "What drawing-pin?"

"That one I lost off the notice-board. It's in your bottle of bath salts."

"What!"

"Yes, I remembered afterwards when we couldn't find it on the floor. I was standing on the bench with your old jar right under my feet. It hadn't got the cork in, you see, so it must have dropped straight in."

"Are you sure? Perhaps it missed the jar and rolled somewhere."

"Not a chance. I searched the whole floor after everybody had gone. Bromwich helped me, and there wasn't a whisker of a drawing-pin anywhere so it's obvious what happened. It doesn't matter, of course. Drawing-pins are cheap enough, but I just thought—" Venables broke off in surprise. Jennings was staring at him with the agonized expression of one who has just bitten into an unexpectedly hot potato. "What's the matter, Jen? What's up?"

Jennings continued to look strained. "What's up!" he echoed. "Something terrible—that's what's up! I've just given the whole jarful to Matron and, what's more, she's going to put them in her bath when she goes to bed to-night."

It took a few moments for the significance of Jennings's remark to sink in. Then the occupants of Dormitory 4 sat up and took notice of all that it implied.

"Yes, I see what you mean," said Venables. "What's going to happen when she sits down!"

"A drawing-pin in the bath-tub! Wow! That's as bad as a crab in a paddling-pool," said Temple.

"Worse," said Darbishire. "The crystals will make the water all cloudy, so she won't see the danger until it gets her."

"She's bound to think you did it on purpose,"

Atkinson pointed out. "She *might* take it as a joke of course, but it's more likely she'll think it's sabotage. Your gruesome revenge because she ticked you off for losing your toothpaste last night."

Jennings was in a quandary. Considered as a practical joke it was a jest in very bad taste; considered as a deliberate act of mischief it would ruin for ever the friendly atmosphere that existed whenever he dropped into the dispensary for a chat. She would never trust him again. Moreover, she would report him to the headmaster for wanton misbehaviour.

"I must warn her at once!" he cried, jumping out of bed and struggling into his slippers. He rushed from the room, down the first flight of stairs and along the landing to the dispensary.

As he approached the door, Mr. Wilkins came round the bend of the corridor on his way to call silence in the top-floor dormitories.

"Jennings! What are you doing out of bed? Go back to your dormitory at once!" he commanded.

"Oh, but sir, I want to see Matron. It's urgent."

"You can't. Dispensary was over ten minutes ago; and in any case she's gone out to supper. She won't be back till late."

Jennings's hand shot to his mouth in sudden realization. Yes, he remembered her saying she was going out! What on earth was to be done?

"What do you want to see her about?" the master asked brusquely.

For a moment Jennings was tempted to explain his

dilemma, but one look at Mr. Wilkins's forbidding expression made him change his mind. Mr. Wilkins would never believe that such a thing could happen by accident: it was such an unlikely story, such a thousand-to-one chance that he would be bound to assume that some diabolical plan was in the process of being hatched.

He could have confessed his problem to Mr. Carter, or even to Mr. Hind—but not to Mr. Wilkins. Old Wilkie wasn't the sort of man to sympathize with third-formers who went about giving grown-ups bottles of extremely painful bath salts.

"It's all right, sir. It doesn't matter," the boy mumbled. He turned and made his way back along the corridor, his brow creased with a worried frown.

"What happened?" his friends demanded when he reached his dormitory.

"Too late; she wasn't there. I've had my chips this time, thanks to you, Venables, you left-footed, butter-fingered clodpoll!"

Angrily, Jennings kicked off his slippers and got into bed. He would have said more, but further comment was ruled out by the arrival of the duty master on his tour of the dormitories.

For some while after Mr. Wilkins had called silence, Jennings lay tossing in his bed while he wracked his brains for some way out of his predicament. Perhaps he should write a warning note and slip it under Matron's door in the hope that she would see it when she returned. It wouldn't be safe to venture downstairs in search of writing materials while the duty master was still on the prowl, of course: he would have to wait until the night-light was switched on on the staircase, and Mr. Wilkins's heavy footfall had ceased to reverberate along the corridors.

Meanwhile there was plenty to think about, and he spent the next twenty minutes composing a suitable note in his mind.

He would start off: *Warning! Beware of the Bath Salts!* in big bold capitals, he decided. Then, underneath: *Do not use, even in an emergency, as Danger Lurks Within.* He was rather pleased with this last phrase and kept repeating it to himself as he thought out what to say next. He could either say: *There is a drawing-pin enclosed, so do not sit or stand, but this is not sabotage as you might think*—or he could omit the explanation and say: *Will see you in the morning and explain all.* Alternatively, he could say . . .

He was still trying to decide which was the best way of phrasing the note when he dropped off to sleep.

At seven o'clock the next morning Jennings was roused by the shrill summons of the rising bell. Immediately, he sat bolt upright, his thoughts focused on the events of the previous evening. Why, oh why, had he fallen asleep at the very moment when he should have been alert and ready for action!

He could have kicked himself! He could have kicked Venables, too, for being so clumsy in the first place, he thought, as he looked round the room at the four sleepers struggling back into wakefulness.

It was too late to go and explain things to Matron.

He would apologize, of course, but by now the damage was done and by breakfast time Mr. Pemberton-Oakes would have heard all about it.

In his mind's eye, Jennings could picture the scene at morning assembly—the headmaster, tall and forbidding on the rostrum: the spine-chilling look in his eye as he said: "Stand up the boy who put the drawing-pin in Matron's bath salts."

Aghast at this horrifying prospect, Jennings called across the room: "Hey, Venables! You'll back me up, won't you! You'll get up and explain to the Head that it was just an accident?"

Venables, still half asleep, couldn't think what Jennings was talking about. When at last he was awake enough to bring his mind to bear on the tragedy he said: "I can't see that it's anything to do with me. *You* gave her the bath salts—*I* didn't."

"Yes, but you dropped the pin in the bottle."

"Ah, but how was I to know what you were going to do with it? If you ask me——"

"Listen," Jennings broke in urgently. "Let's both get dressed at supersonic speed and see if we can catch Matron before she goes off to report me to the Head. We may just do it, if we're quick."

With this in mind, Jennings sprang out of bed and threw his clothes on with all possible speed. "No time to wash," he muttered as he wove his way into his shirt. His haste was so great that he thrust both feet through one leg of his shorts and several seconds were lost while he untangled the muddle.

Then he was ready. "Come on!" he cried—and looked across the room to see Venables, still sitting on his bed in his pyjama trousers. "Oh, for goodness' sake, Ven!" he protested. "I thought you were going to help me."

Venables stretched, yawned, got up and reached under the bed for his sandals. "All right, but don't rush me. I'm not properly awake yet."

"But there's no time!" Jennings danced with impatience. "Matron will be hopping mad this morning, after what happened to her last night. She may even be——"

But Venables wasn't listening. He was standing by his bed examining the crêpe sole of one of his sandals with deep interest. Then he looked up and said: "I say, that's funny. That's very funny indeed!"

"Huh! I'm glad *you* think something's funny, because *I* don't," snorted Jennings. "Here I am up to my eyebrows in trouble and you——"

"Oh, but it *is* funny. I've just made a discovery," Venables interrupted. "That drawing-pin didn't drop into the bath-salt bottle after all. I've just found it stuck in the sole of my sandal."

"What!"

"Yes, here it is, look." Venables prised the pin out with his finger-nails and stood looking at it as though it were a jewel of great price. "I must have trodden on it point upwards when I jumped down off the bench, and I've been walking round with it stuck in my shoe ever since. No wonder I couldn't find it!"

There was a burst of laughter from the adjoining beds as Darbishire, Temple and Atkinson savoured the joke.

Jennings did not join in. His mind was reeling with shock. All his anxieties on Matron's behalf; all the restless tossing until sleep overcame him; all the nightmare speculations about morning assembly . . . And he needn't have bothered!

He crossed to the wash-basins, selected the largest sponge he could find and held it under the cold tap.

"You must admit it had its funny side, Jen," urged Temple, still chortling as he stripped his bed.

"Oh, yes, very funny indeed!" Jennings replied in a tense, strained voice.

Then he hurled the dripping wet sponge at Venables and caught him squarely on the nose. The victim gasped and grabbed for a towel as streams of cold water coursed down his bare chest and soaked the top of his pyjama trousers.

"Very funny indeed," Jennings repeated. "But not," he added as he made for the door, "not half so funny as Venables looks now!"

CHAPTER 10

# *Change of Plan*

IT WAS NOT until the end of the following week that Jennings and Darbishire were released from their daily chore of rolling the cricket square and tidying the headmaster's garden.

"Thank goodness this lark's nearly over," Jennings said to Darbishire during their last rolling session on Saturday morning. "I reckon I know every blade of grass by sight from one end of the pitch to the other. And as for this tinny old roller clanking along behind us like a lorry-load of milk churns, I can almost hear it in my sleep."

"You should try not to think about it," Darbishire advised. "Be like me and keep your mind on other things—it makes the time go quicker."

"What sort of other things?"

"Things to look forward to. Like, say, for instance, a moment ago, I was just thinking that if old Pettigrew does his stuff on Monday we could have a special private stamp exhibition on Tuesday with everyone queueing up to see ye new two-and-a-half *p Scientific Inventions of the Twentieth Century*, by kind permission of Messrs. Jennings and Darbishire."

"Wow! Yes of course—Monday! I'd forgotten it was

so soon," said Jennings. "I promised to let Petters have cash in advance before he goes home to-day. Got your money handy?"

Originally, the boys had spoken airily of buying a whole sheet of the new stamps when they were issued. But by this stage of the term their bank balances were so low that this scheme had to be abandoned and they had been obliged to settle for a single two-and-a-half pence stamp apiece.

"Actually, this will make them a lot rarer," Jennings had explained when lack of funds had forced them to revise their grandiose plans. "I read an article in your stamp mag. about crafty collectors who actually destroy genuine, rare specimens in order to make the ones that are left even rarer."

"But these won't be really *rare.* Anyone can buy them," Darbishire had objected.

"Not anyone in Form 3! At least, not until it's too late to get them with Monday's post-mark on—and after that it doesn't count."

Though willing to help, Pettigrew was not keen to put himself to any trouble when Jennings handed him five pence in coppers after school that morning.

"So long as it doesn't make me late," he said, slipping the money into his pocket. "I like to get here by twenty to nine, so I've got time for cricket on the quad before assembly."

"You'll have bags of time," Jennings assured him. "You be on the doorstep at half past eight when the post office opens: it'll only take you five minutes to bike up to school from the village. You'll be able to play a whole series of test matches before the bell goes at ten to."

Sunday passed without incident, and on Monday morning Jennings awoke with a feeling of joyful anticipation.

Not so Darbishire, who woke up with a slight headache! "I think I'll go and see Matron after breakfast and get some aspirins or something," he said to his friend as they stood at the wash-basins together, just after the rising bell.

"You can't go till we've had a look at our new stamps," Jennings replied with the intolerance of one who happens to be feeling perfectly fit. "You can go up to Dispensary afterwards. You'll have masses of time. She goes on doling out pills and stuff right up till first lesson—even later sometimes."

"The later the better, if there's a chance of missing first lesson," Darbishire observed. "It's old Wilkie's maths test this morning, and I reckon people with headaches shouldn't be allowed in."

Darbishire agreed to defer his visit to Matron, for he was as keen as Jennings to inspect the new issue; and as soon as breakfast was over the two philatelists went off to the bicycle shed to await the day boy's arrival.

They didn't have to wait long. At eight thirty-two there was a scrunch of tyres on the gravel and the keenly-awaited cyclist wobbled to a stop and dismounted by the door.

"Got them?" Jennings asked eagerly.

Pettigrew shook his head. "Your Intelligence Service is a bit off the beam," he reported. "You told me the post office opened at half past eight."

"Well?"

"It doesn't. It opens at quarter to nine. I'd been cooling my heels outside for quite a time before somebody came along and told me."

Jennings was aghast at the failure of his plans. "Couldn't you have waited?" he cried. "If you'd hung on till they were open you could still have been here before assembly, if you'd put a jerk on."

Pettigrew thought this unreasonable, and said so. Having stretched a point and left home early, he was not prepared to stretch another one and arrive at school late. Well, not just for something like a couple of mouldy stamps, he told them. Not being a collector himself, he really couldn't see why chaps should get so steamed up about the subject. After all, these weren't even *foreign* stamps: any old body could buy them at any old post office. And besides, he went on, he particularly wanted to get to school in good time that morning because . . .

Jennings wasn't interested in Pettigrew's excuses or in his views on philately. The only thought in his mind was that his whole brilliant scheme was in ruins.

"Come on, Darbi!" he said with a snort of frustration. "We might have known we couldn't expect much help from a bat-brained, shrimp-witted clodpoll like Petters. He's so ignorant he doesn't even know one side of a foreign stamp from the other."

Pettigrew acknowledged the insults with a disarming smile. "Philately will get you nowhere," he observed blandly.

"Why won't it? Of course it will! Actually it teaches you a lot about——"

"Oh, belt up!" said Pettigrew in resigned tones. "I was just making a joke only you were too dim-witted to see it. There were these two Chinese philatelists, you see, and one was flattering the other about his stamp collection only he couldn't pronounce his *r*'s velly plopelly, so when the first one tried to say, 'flattery will get you nowhere', he said——"

"*You* belt up for a change," Jennings broke in. "A fine time to start cracking feeble jokes when you've just ruined our whole day and gummed up our *Scientific Inventions of the Twentieth Century*." He swung round and flounced angrily away with Darbishire trailing behind him.

Jennings was feeling too disappointed to discuss the matter when they got indoors. "That's that, then," he said with a shrug. "You can go up and see Matron now and get your head shrunk, or whatever it is you want."

"Actually, my headache's a bit better now," Darbishire admitted. "At least, it was until old Pettigrew double-crossed us. That made me so furious I've probably got blood pressure now, instead."

"Better go and see her anyway," Jennings advised. "If you're lucky she may decide you're too ill for Sir's maths test. Remember old Bromo, that time?"

Darbishire nodded. Some weeks earlier Bromwich,

having confessed to his friends that he hadn't bothered to look at his revision prep., had gone off to the dispensary with a vague, unspecified malady, at the very moment that Mr. Wilkins had arranged to test Form 3's knowledge of French verbs. Instead of sending him back into class, Matron had allowed the patient to sit quietly in a comfortable chair in the sick-room for the rest of the morning.

The treatment was almost magical in its effect; for as soon as the bell rang for the end of school the invalid jumped up and announced that the cure was complete and that he was now bursting with rude health. In proof of this he went downstairs, ate an enormous lunch and scored forty-three runs for his side in that afternoon's cricket game.

"If old Bromo can get away with it, so can you," Jennings said.

Darbishire was deeply shocked at such an unworthy suggestion. "Oh, but I wouldn't do a thing like that, just to get out of class," he protested. "My case is quite different. I've got a genuine, king-sized, jumbo-jet of a headache—at least I *think* I have!"

He shook his head by way of experiment and drew a painful breath. "If it was left to me, of course, I'd probably just suffer in silence, but I suppose I'd better go and report, seeing that you're so insistent."

He crossed to the staircase and climbed with slow and careful footsteps, like a delicate invalid who has been warned not to overtax his strength.

Jennings wandered off in the opposite direction,

brooding in gloomy silence over the morning's disaster, and trying to decide which form of medieval torture would be hideous enough to inflict upon Pettigrew as a revenge for his treachery.

He was passing the masters' common room when the door opened and Mr. Wilkins looked out.

"Ah, Jennings! Can I trust you to carry out an extremely simple, yet urgent mission without making a mess of it?" the master asked with heavy humour.

"Yes, sir. Of course, sir."

Mr. Wilkins handed him an envelope, stamped, addressed and ready for despatch. "I want this letter posted, right away, if you'll be so kind," he said.

The staff room door closed, leaving Jennings standing in the corridor frowning over the envelope in his hand.

The arrangements for posting outgoing mail at Linbury Court School were well known to everyone concerned. When stamped, letters were placed in a wire basket in the front hall which Robinson emptied each day at five o'clock when he took the post down to the village in time for the evening collection. This was the normal procedure and was clearly what Mr. Wilkins had in mind. On rare occasions, however, when the basket had already been cleared, a master might send a boy direct to the post office with a letter which had missed the collection in the hall.

Mr. Wilkins had said he wanted the letter *posted*, Jennings reminded himself, and had said that he wanted it done *right away* . . . Well, why not! By contriving to misunderstand the master's intentions he could post it at the post office, and use the opportunity to buy the new stamps which Pettigrew had so treacherously failed to obtain.

Jennings's frown deepened. There would be trouble if he was found out—even though Mr. Wilkins had unwittingly left him a loophole. Was the loophole large enough to escape through in case of need? A great deal depended upon that!

He glanced at his watch. The post office would be open in five minutes' time, and the bell for assembly would be sounding in ten. If he was absent from assembly it might be assumed that he was upstairs in Matron's dispensary queueing up for—for—well, there were a dozen reasons, from cough mixture to new shoe laces, to explain why a boy might be detained in Matron's room during the morning assembly.

The testing time would come at nine o'clock when they all went into class and the register was called. If he wasn't back by then his absence was sure to be noticed . . . And he couldn't possibly do the journey to the post office and back, *and* buy his stamps in the time available, not even if he ran full speed all the way.

So the idea was a wash-out after all! Unless—unless . . . His eyes brightened with inspiration. Why go on foot, when Pettigrew's bicycle was in the shed just beyond the side door! Considering how he had failed them in their hour of need, it was only fair, Jennings reasoned, that Pettigrew should make some contribution to the task on hand. His bicycle would be just the job for cutting ten minutes off the journey time. He would ask permission to borrow the machine when he got back. He couldn't afford to hang about looking for the owner with time so short.

The decision was made: he would go at once, leaving and returning by the less-frequented gate at the far end of the grounds. It was unlikely that any master would notice him if he took that route, and in any case the track was screened by bushes for most of its length.

Should he tell Darbishire he was going? No, there wasn't time! He slipped Mr. Wilkins's letter into his blazer pocket and hurried out through the side door. As he went, his mind was busy making out a mental time-table of the operation:

8.45 Bike to post office, *via* back gate.

8.50 Arrive P.O. Post letter and buy new issue.

8.55 Return to school.

9.00 Join Form 3 crocodile coming out of assembly.

It all seemed so easy. With a foolproof plan like this in his mind, he could hardly go wrong!

Pettigrew's machine was in the bicycle rack just by the door. Jennings wheeled it outside and, avoiding the early morning cricketers on the playing field, walked with it till he was safely past the entrance to the kitchen yard. Over by the tool-shed he could see Robinson tinkering with a roll of wire netting, but he was engrossed in his work and didn't look up as the boy passed across his line of vision.

After a last cautious look round, Jennings scooted

the machine into action, flung his leg over the saddle and pedalled off down the dusty track as fast as his legs could rotate.

* * * *

The dispensary was empty when Darbishire arrived, and the first thing that caught his eye was a small stack of clinical thermometers propped up in a glass tumbler on the trolley-wagon.

Matron would be certain to take his temperature, he thought. And if he had a headache, surely he ought to have a temperature to go with it, or she might think he was malingering. Had he got a temperature? He wasn't sure: but if he *hadn't* she'd send him into school, so the best thing to do was to make sure that he had a high one.

He took one of the thermometers from the tumbler and crossed to the wash-basin where he turned on the hot tap and held the glass tube underneath for some seconds. A quick glance showed that the column of mercury was rising, but he kept the instrument under the tap for a little longer to be on the safe side. Then he heard footsteps approaching the door, so he rushed across the room and sat down.

When Matron entered a few moments later, she found her patient sitting with a thermometer in his mouth and a look of deep suffering on his face.

"Hullo, Darbishire. What's the matter with you?" she greeted him.

"I've got a headache, Matron," he mumbled.

"Too bad. Is that all?"

"Well, I—er—I just thought I might have got a temperature, as well."

"We'll soon see about that." She removed the thermometer and examined it. Then she said: "H'm! I don't know whether to send for the vet or the undertaker."

The patient gulped. "What do you mean, Matron?" he faltered.

"Well, I suppose a fire-breathing dragon on a diet of brimstone and North Sea gas might be as hot-blooded as this; but no human being could have a temperature of a hundred-and-ten and stay alive for long."

Darbishire looked down at the toes of his shoes. A hundred-and-ten! He'd bungled things badly. "Well—I—er—" he began.

"Don't bother to explain. I've met this little dodge often enough before." She indicated the wash-basin across the room. "Besides, you forgot to turn the hot tap off when you'd finished warming up the thermometer."

Acutely embarrassed, Darbishire muttered: "Yes, Matron: sorry, Matron. Actually, I *have* got a headache but I can't prove it, so I thought——"

"You don't need to *prove* it," she broke in. "I can see you're looking a bit peaky this morning and I'm the best judge of what's to be done about it."

She took his temperature again—which turned out to be normal—gave him a small dose of aspirin for his headache and told him to sit down quietly in the sick-room until morning break.

"You don't think I ought to see the doctor, too, Matron?" the boy suggested hopefully. "He comes on Monday mornings, doesn't he?"

"Yes, but you're not nearly ill enough to waste Dr. Furnival's time," she told him.

Darbishire looked uncomfortable. "I know, Matron: it's only that, when I go back into school, the chaps may think I was just pretending if it wasn't serious enough for the doctor, because we've got a test this morning and——"

Her laugh drowned the rest of his excuse. "Don't try my patience too far, Darbishire, or I may change my mind and send you into school just as Mr. Wilkins is writing up the first question."

He forced a wan smile and walked off to the sick-room with the brave step of an invalid clinging on to life by sheer will-power and a small dose of aspirin.

CHAPTER 11

# *Cycle of Events*

AT TEN MINUTES to nine when the bell was ringing for assembly and Darbishire was sitting quietly in the sick-room, Jennings was pedalling briskly along the village street. He drew up outside the Linbury General Stores and Post Office and propped Pettigrew's bicycle against the wall of the shop.

So far, he was right up to schedule; and provided there wasn't a queue at the post office counter he could look forward to being in and out again in a matter of moments.

He started towards the door, and then stopped suddenly as the youthful, sandy-haired figure of the local doctor strode out of the shop and got into his car.

Jennings turned his back and studied the display of goods in the window with close attention. Dr. Furnival had a branch surgery in the village and was also medical officer to Linbury Court School. It might have been safe to say "good morning", for the doctor had only a vague knowledge of school routine; and, in any case, Jennings was carrying Mr. Wilkins's letter as his passport to freedom.

On the other hand, it would be better not to draw attention to himself, the boy decided. Dr. Furnival would be visiting the school that morning, as he always did on Mondays, and might stop for a chat with the headmaster. Some chance remark about seeing a boy in the village might well unearth a clue that was better left undisturbed.

As it happened the danger was soon past, for Dr. Furnival drove off down the street without a backward glance, and as soon as he had gone Jennings hurried in through the shop door.

The post office was at the far end, beyond the provisions and tinned-food counter on the left, and the mouse-traps, cornplasters and egg-whisks which made up the hardware department on the other side of the shop.

Already there were half a dozen customers in front of him waiting to buy the new stamp issue, but as the queue seemed to be moving briskly Jennings was not unduly worried. He joined on to the end of the line and groped in his pocket for his money.

Then came the shock . . . His pocket was empty . . . ! He had forgotten to demand the return of the vital five pence in coppers from the faithless Pettigrew!

For some seconds the boy stood at the tail of the queue scolding himself in exasperation. He must be mad, he told himself severely! He needed his brains testing! As a master-planner he was about as much use as a clockwork orange! How *could* he have forgotten the vital factor on which his whole scheme had depended!

He searched through his pockets, although he knew before he started that he wouldn't find any money in them. But what he *did* find amongst the grey fluff and toffee papers in his blazer was the crumpled stamp he had been saving for the next time he wrote to his Aunt Angela. He pressed it flat with his fingers, picked off the grey fluff and examined it carefully. There wasn't much gum left on the back, but it could probably be made to stick. Anyway, it was, without question, a genuine unused postage stamp to the value of two-and-a-half pence. Would they be willing to exchange it for a specimen of the new issue costing the same amount? He could but try!

By this time the customers in front of him had departed and Jennings found himself at the head of the queue. With some diffidence he put his stamp on the counter and said: "Good morning. Would you be kind enough to change this for a two-and-a-half *p Scientific Inventions of the Twentieth Century*, please?"

"Are you joking!" said the young woman behind the counter.

"No, honestly! But, you see, I've accidentally left my money at home—or rather I haven't actually *left* it, but I gave it to somebody who's still got it, because I didn't remember to ask him for it back. And this stamp's perfectly all right: it's worth two-and-a-half pence because it's never been used."

She pushed it back across the counter. "Sorry, nothing doing."

"Oh, but surely——" Jennings was prepared to argue his case. "It's terribly urgent. You see, I really wanted two of the new issue, one for me and one for my friend, but if we could have just *one* it would be better than nothing because——"

There were restless stirrings in the queue behind him and the young woman said: "You're wasting time, son, and I'm busy. There's a dozen customers waiting to be served—people who've actually remembered to bring their money with them."

Accepting defeat, the boy picked up his stamp and made his way back through the shop. The queue had grown considerably since his arrival, and at the end of the line he saw Miss Thorpe waiting to be served.

"Good morning! Good morning!" she trilled like a thrush greeting the dawn. "Splendid news about the pig, wasn't it! He's ever so happy out at East Brinkington. Mr. Nutt treats him just like one of the family."

Jennings smiled, mumbled politely and was about to pass on, but Miss Thorpe was in one of her talkative moods. "I can't think why the post office is so crowded at this early hour of the morning," she twittered. "There's never a soul about when I come in at this time, as a rule."

"It's the *Scientific Inventions of the Twentieth Century*," he told her.

"*What* scientific inventions of the twentieth century? Surely we've got enough in the Stores already, what with the bacon-slicer and the deep-freeze cabinet. What next? We're not going to have our bills made out by computer, are we?"

Patiently, Jennings explained: "It's a new issue of stamps on sale. These people in front are buying them so that they can get them postmarked with to-day's date."

"Good gracious me, what an extraordinary thing to do!" Miss Thorpe and the freckle-faced Pettigrew had one thing in common—neither was interested in collecting stamps. "What a nuisance, having to queue up like this, but what else can you do when the stamp machine is empty," she grumbled. "I'm late for Playgroup already and it's my turn to get the equipment out; but I simply *must* get this letter off by the morning collection." She waved an envelope in the air by way of demonstration.

It was a good chance and Jennings seized it. "You want to buy a stamp? Just an ordinary one?"

"I certainly do. I don't mind how ordinary it is, so long as I don't have to queue up half the morning to buy it."

He offered her the crumpled stamp. "It hasn't got much gum on the back, but it'll stick if you press it hard enough."

Miss Thorpe was delighted. She gave him the two-and-a-half pence she had ready in her hand, took the stamp and hurried off to post her letter.

Jennings found a place in the queue, and in five minutes' time was again confronting the young woman behind the counter.

She was surprised to see him back. "You again! Won the pools or robbed a bank?" she inquired with mock interest as she swept up the coins and handed him the stamp he had risked so much to acquire.

If only he'd been able to afford *two* specimens, he thought as he turned away from the counter! Miss Thorpe would probably have been only too pleased to lend him the extra money, but he hadn't thought of asking her until it was too late. So what about old Darbishire? They couldn't stick one stamp in two stamp albums. Should they toss up for it?

At that moment he caught sight of the post office clock and forgot everything except the need to get back to school without wasting another moment.

It was nearly five past nine. Zero hour was already past and he was still half a mile away from his base. Jennings rushed out of the stores, dropped Mr. Wilkins' letter in the post-box, grabbed the bicycle and pedalled back along the village street as fast as he could.

They would all be in class by now, he reminded himself, as he tore past the vicarage garden: Mr. Wilkins would have called the register and found out that he was missing, so there was bound to be trouble one way or another.

Rotten old Pettigrew! he thought, as the pedals whirled round faster and faster . . . And daft old me, he added, remembering his precious five pence still in the day boy's pocket.

* * * *

As it happened, Mr. Wilkins was not calling the register when Jennings was setting off on his return journey. Instead, he was still standing on the threshold of

Classroom 3 listening to Pettigrew complaining that his bicycle had been stolen.

"Stolen! Nonsense, boy, how could it have been stolen," he was saying in disbelieving tones. "You've probably left it somewhere else."

"No sir, honestly!" There was no mistaking the anxiety in the day boy's voice. "I left it in the rack in the bike shed when I went to play on the quad; and when I went back to get my books out of the saddle-bag just now, it had gone."

"That's quite right, sir. I can prove it," added Marshall, another day boy, who had arrived at school by bicycle shortly after his friend. "Pettigrew was talking to Jennings and Darbishire outside the bike shed when I got here, and his bike was definitely in the rack then. I know, because I caught my pedal in his spokes when I was trying to get past."

Mr. Wilkins fretted with impatience. He was anxious to get on with the maths test. "Come and see me at break. I'll get some boys to help you have a look round for it," he said.

"Oh, but sir!" Pettigrew was almost distraught. "It'll be too late then; the thief will be miles away."

"But there *isn't* a thief, you silly little boy! It's been moved, that's all. How could anyone steal it from the bicycle shed without being seen?"

Form 3, sitting in their desks agog with excitement, were quick to suggest possible theories.

"Someone could have sneaked up the drive while we were all in assembly, sir," suggested Atkinson.

"Yes sir: he could have been pretending to sell brushes or to read the gas meter or something," added Martin-Jones who liked his mysteries to be as complicated as possible. "Disguised with a beard and dark glasses. Or, say, wearing an old slouch hat, pretending to sell bootlaces, with the brim pulled down over his eyes."

"And he could have had a fast car waiting at the end of the drive to make his get-away," said Rumbelow.

"He wouldn't need a car; he'd got a bicycle," Bromwich pointed out.

"All right, then—a fast bicycle," Rumbelow conceded. "And he could put the police off the scent by throwing away his old slouch hat——"

"Quiet!" boomed Mr. Wilkins. He had enough to think about without listening to fantastic theories about slouch-hatted meter-readers on fast bicycles with bootlaces pulled down over their eyes—or whatever it was the silly little boys were prattling about.

In his opinion it was unlikely that the machine had been stolen, but if this should prove to be the case, then the theft must be reported to the police without delay. First of all, he would have to make quite sure of the facts. To the class he said: "You boys carry on revising for the maths test till I get back. Come along, Pettigrew," he added, as he swept out of the room. "You come with me and show me exactly where this bicycle was standing when you last saw it."

It was now twelve minutes past nine. As master and

boy reached the ground floor and crossed the hall, they met Jennings proceeding in the opposite direction. Mechanically, Mr. Wilkins said: "Quickly, Jennings! You're late for class."

"Yes, sir. Just going up now, sir."

Mr. Wilkins, with other things on his mind, did not pursue the matter. At a brisk pace he led the way out through the side door, and a few moments later they reached the bicycle shed . . . The first thing they saw was Pettigrew's bicycle neatly parked in the rack.

The owner was delighted. "Oh, sir, look, sir! It's come back. How super!" He did a little dance to demonstrate his joy and relief, but Mr. Wilkins did not join in.

"Is this the machine you reported as having been stolen?" the master demanded suspiciously.

"Oh, yes, sir. This is my bike, all right, sir." Pettigrew thumped the saddle in proof of ownership. "I can't think what's happened. I know it wasn't here when I looked after assembly."

"Don't be ridiculous, boy. It must have been here all the time. Bicycles can't walk."

"No, I know, sir. I just can't explain it. It's just a great big mystery, sir, if you ask me."

Mr. Wilkins was not prepared to hang about in the bicycle shed solving mysteries while Form 3, with no master in charge, were wasting the lesson in idle chat and flicking paper pellets across the desks.

"Upstairs!" he ordered curtly. "We'll straighten out this nonsense when we get into the classroom."

CHAPTER 12

# *Gesture of Goodwill*

JENNINGS WAS SITTING quietly at his desk when Mr. Wilkins and Pettigrew returned to the classroom shortly after quarter past nine. He had learned with relief that the attendance register had not yet been called, for it meant that he would not have to use the excuse he had prepared to cover his absence. Though true in all respects, it complied with the letter of the law rather than the spirit, and would have sounded a somewhat flimsy pretext if Mr. Wilkins had decided to investigate the matter in detail.

But though Jennings was sitting quietly, the rest of Form 3 were *not*; and as the form master entered the room he was aware of a hubbub of chatter and the scurry of feet scampering back to unoccupied desks. Form 3 had been enjoying the unexpected break from routine and were sorry that it had not lasted longer.

"Did you catch the burglar, sir?" Atkinson asked with a giggle.

"That was hardly likely, considering that the bicycle was there all the time," Mr. Wilkins retorted, coldly.

"Oh, jolly good sir! Still it was worth going downstairs to make sure, wasn't it!"

Nods and smiles of agreement all round the room suggested that any sort of time-wasting procedure was well worth the effort if it delayed the start of the morning's work.

Mr. Wilkins glowered. "This is no joking matter. Thanks to the monumental idiocy of Pettigrew, we have lost twenty minutes of our maths test."

"Good old Petters," Martin-Jones whispered softly—but not softly enough to escape the sharp ears of Mr. Wilkins.

That did it!

"Right! As this form obviously approves of Pettigrew's delaying tactics in luring me out to the bicycle shed by false pretences, we will hold the maths test this afternoon, instead of playing cricket."

From being the hero, Pettigrew suddenly became the villain of the piece as the class rounded on him in hostility.

"Pettigrew! Rotten old Pettigrew," they jeered in voiceless whispers. "Fancy playing a low-down trick like that on Mr. Wilkins! . . . And now we've got to suffer for it! . . . We don't want to lose our cricket just because of you."

The day boy was shattered by the injustice of the attack. "Oh but sir, it wasn't my fault, honestly," he protested. "I thought my bike *had* been stolen, really I did."

"Nonsense," said Mr. Wilkins. "The whole thing was a deliberate conspiracy."

"No, it wasn't, sir. You don't understand—I mean, *I*

don't understand how it happened. It's all a mystery because——" Pettigrew floundered to a stop, and Jennings, seated in the back row, decided that in the interests of justice the cause of the mystery would have to be revealed. It wasn't fair to let old Pettigrew take the blame for something that wasn't his fault even though he—J. C. T. Jennings—would find himself with some awkward questions to answer. It seemed that his flimsy excuse would have to be tried out after all.

He put up his hand and said: "Sir, please, sir, I took Pettigrew's bike out of the bike shed just before assembly, sir: and I put it back again afterwards."

Mr. Wilkins bridled indignantly. "Why? A practical joke?"

"No sir, I borrowed it to ride down to the village."

"You did *what*!" The master stared at the boy in bewilderment. "And may I ask who in the name of thunder gave you permission to go cycling off to the village during morning assembly?"

"You did, sir."

"*I* did! Don't be ridiculous, boy. I never did anything of the sort. If this is another attempt to——"

"Oh, but you did, sir," Jennings broke in. "You gave me a letter and told me to go and post it immediately. And I only borrowed Pettigrew's bike so I could be back in time for the maths test, sir."

Mr. Wilkins clasped his hand to his brow. "But, you—you silly little boy, Jennings, I didn't mean you to post it in the *post office*. I expected you to put it in the basket in the hall."

A look of comprehension dawned slowly on Jennings's face. "Oh, I *see*, sir. So *that's* what you meant! Yes, I see now, I do indeed. That was stupid of me!" He shook his head in self-reproach. "Still, you *did* say you wanted it posted *at once*. Urgent mission, you said it was, sir; and if I hadn't taken it to the post office it would still be sitting there in the basket until five o'clock this afternoon, wouldn't it, sir!"

There was a pause while Mr. Wilkins digested the information. In point of fact he had every reason to be grateful to Jennings, for the speedy delivery of his letter was a matter of some importance. Indeed, he would have gone to the post office himself to catch the early collection if he had had time before assembly. Now, thanks to the boy's flair for misunderstanding instructions, the letter was certain to reach its destination first thing the following morning.

Mr. Wilkins made no further comment until he had marked the attendance register. Then he laid down his pen and said: "After giving the matter due thought, I would agree that it would hardly be fair for me to punish the whole form for an offence for which I assumed Pettigrew was responsible. In the same way, it would not be fair for me to punish Pettigrew for doing something which Jennings now admits was his fault. By the same token, it would not be fair for me to punish Jennings, now I know that he was misguidedly trying to carry out my instructions to the best of his limited ability."

By this time Form 3 were becoming confused as to who was being held responsible for what.

"Does that mean we shan't be having the maths test instead of cricket this afternoon?" Venables asked hopefully.

"Precisely that," Mr. Wilkins agreed. "As we have already lost so much of the lesson we will defer the test until this time next week. That should make everybody happy except, perhaps——" He glanced down the attendance register, noting the name of the only absentee. "Except, perhaps, Darbishire. He will be disappointed to learn, when he returns from the sick-room, that he won't have succeeded in dodging the maths test after all."

There was still a little while left before the end of the period and Mr. Wilkins was determined to see that the time was not wasted.

"We'll have a look at the Theorem of Pythagoras, since we've got a few minutes in hand," he said, picking up the chalk. "It's a most useful and practical piece of geometry, so copy down this diagram in your note books."

On the blackboard he drew a right-angled triangle and marked out a square on each of the three sides. He was adding the construction lines when Temple asked him: "How d'you mean, it's useful, sir? It just looks like a lopsided windmill to me."

Mr. Wilkins completed his diagram and turned from the board. "This is a triangle with a right angle at its apex," he explained. "This square which I have drawn on the side opposite to the right angle, which is called the hypotenuse, is equal in area to the two smaller squares on the other two sides, added together."

Temple still looked blank. "But you said it was useful, sir," he persisted. "I still don't see what you can make it do."

Patiently, Mr. Wilkins said: "It's useful, Temple, because if you understand the principle on which the theorem is based, it enables you to—for example—mark out a tennis court or a football pitch and to be quite sure that you've got the corners set at the proper angle." He glanced at his watch: it was nearly time for the bell. "Everybody write this down under the figure you've just drawn: The Theorem of Pythagoras——"

"Sir, please, sir can we do it in rough?" asked Atkinson.

"You should never do anything *in rough*," the master reproved. "But you can use abbreviations if you like because we haven't got much time." At a brisk pace he dictated: "In a right-angled triangle, the square on the hypotenuse is equal to the sum of the squares on the other two sides."

"Please, sir, how do you spell hypotenuse? It is two ——?"

But the bell for the end of the lesson drowned Bromwich's question.

"All got that down?" Mr. Wilkins boomed above the sound of the bell. "I'll go through it again to-morrow afternoon. Meanwhile, have a look at it during prep to-night and see if you can work out what it means."

The next lesson was English with Mr. Carter, but Jennings's mind was not wholly concentrated on his work. He sat staring at his book while he thought about other things.

He had weathered the storm of Mr. Wilkins' wrath over his journey to the village far better than he had dared to hope—and, indeed, far better than he had deserved. He was grateful to Fate for letting him off so lightly, particularly as he was now the proud owner of a stamp that had caused him so much trouble to acquire.

But what about Darbishire suffering in the sick-room with no stamp to look forward to when he came down! Poor old Darbi, he thought. He didn't know yet that his friend had succeeded against overwhelming odds in getting hold of a specimen of the new issue. He didn't even know about the jumbo-jet of a hoo-hah that had been going on in his absence—the race against the clock, the near disaster of the missing five pence, the alleged bicycle theft, and Mr. Wilkins' kindly tolerance in not asking too many awkward questions.

A kind Fate and a kind-hearted Mr. Wilkins! Jennings felt a warm glow of happiness inside him and suddenly decided to let Darbishire have the two-and-a-half pence *Scientific Inventions of the Twentieth Century* all to himself.

Well, why not? he thought, basking in his glow of happiness. He could almost feel a halo floating a few inches above his head. It would be a sacrifice of course —a gesture of goodwill. Old Darbi would be as chuffed as two coots. And talk about a surprise! He might even . . .

"Jennings, what have I just been saying?" Mr. Carter's voice cut across the boy's flight of fancy and brought him down to earth with a bump.

"Er—do you mean just now, sir?" he asked, playing for time.

"Of course, I mean just now. It would be asking too much of Form 3—and Jennings, in particular—to expect anyone to remember what I'd told them the term before last."

Jennings's face was a mask of concentration. "Oh, yes, I *was* listening sir, but I just didn't happen to catch the very last thing you said."

"I'm not surprised. You've been sunk in a deep trance for the last ten minutes." Mr. Carter heaved a sigh of resignation. "For your information, Jennings, I was reading to the form an extract from a poem by Wordsworth about duty and self-sacrifice."

"Ah, yes sir, I remember now. It's just come back to me . . . Wordsworth—duty and self-sacrifice."

Jennings beamed Mr. Carter a disarming smile. It was meant to suggest that there wasn't much about duty and self-sacrifice that the poet Wordsworth could teach a chap who had just decided to give away his latest, most treasured possession.

* * * *

Darbishire came down from the sick-room during morning break, his headache completely cured. Jennings met him coming through the side door on to the quad.

"Hullo, Darbi, are you better?" Jennings fished in his blazer pocket and produced an old tobacco tin given to him by Mr. Carter. "I've got something for you in here. It's a present."

"For me!" Darbishire was nonplussed. Presents from Jennings were a rare occurrence. "It's funny you should say that because I've got a present for you."

"Honestly?"

"Yes, of course." From his blazer pocket Darbishire produced a folded sheet of paper torn from the dispensary telephone pad. "It's something you'll be jolly pleased with, I can tell you."

"So is yours," Jennings assured him. "And you'll never guess what it is. Not in a million years you wouldn't guess. You'd say it was impossible. Actually, it's a sort of sacrifice, as you might say."

Beaming with goodwill, Jennings exchanged the sacrificial tobacco tin for the folded message form. Both boys looked inside their containers and took out their gifts.

Then they stared at each other in stunned amazement. Each was holding between his fingers an unused, two-and-a-half pence *Scientific Inventions of the Twentieth Century* stamp.

Darbishire was the first to recover from the shock. "Where did you get it from?" he demanded.

Jennings waved his hand vaguely. "It's a long story. I'll tell you later. Where did you get yours?"

"From Dr. Furnival. I was sitting there in the sick-room when he went through with Matron. He asked me if I collected stamps. And when I said yes, he told me he'd just bought some of the new issue."

"Oh, I see!" So *that* was what Dr. Furnival had been doing in the post office! It all fitted in. "And then, I suppose, he gave you a stamp to cure your headache."

"Well, not exactly, but he gave me one, anyway. Decent of him, wasn't it!"

Jennings heaved a sigh. All the trouble he had taken to get hold of his specimen, while old Darbi had just sat around in an easy-chair and had it dropped into his lap without having to lift a finger! Tut! Some chaps had jam on everything!

"And then I thought I'd very decently give it to you, seeing that you wouldn't have a chance of getting one yourself," Darbishire went on. "Still, I needn't have bothered as it happens. It's crazy really, because we could both have kept our own and we'd be just as well off."

Jennings shook his head. "Oh no! It's much better this way. There wouldn't have been any sacrifice if we'd done that. Like old Wordsworth was nattering about."

"*Who?*"

"Mr. Carter read us one of his poems in English," Jennings explained.

"I didn't know Mr. Carter had written any poems in English."

"Not *Mr. Carter's* poems, you clodpoll—old *Wordsworth's*. And I didn't mean a poem in English, either."

"No? What language did he write it in, then?"

Jennings clicked his teeth in exasperation. Really, old Darbishire could be thick-headed when the mood took him! Patiently, he said: "During our English lesson, Mr. Carter read us a poem by this geezer, Wordsworth, about duty and self-sacrifice and what decent things they were. So now we've both given each other our one and only new issue without knowing we were going to get one back, we've both made a sort of sacrifice."

Darbishire nodded. "That ought to please old Wordsworth."

"Not half so much as it pleases me," said Jennings. "When you went up to Dispensary we hadn't a hope of getting even *one* stamp between us. Now we've got two, thanks to our self-sacrifice. Come on, let's go and write envelopes to ourselves and stick the stamps on."

The bell for the end of break rang while they were still ferreting through their desks in search of their writing-pads, and it was not until the rest period in the library after the midday meal that they had time to cope with important philatelic business.

Then, Jennings wrote an envelope addressed to J. C. T. Jennings, Linbury Court School, Linbury, Sussex, England, and stuck the new issue stamp in the top right-hand corner.

"It seems crazy sending an empty envelope through the post," he remarked. "Waste of two-and-a-half *p*."

"That's what I thought," Darbishire agreed from the next table. "So I've written a letter to myself to put inside. Only a short one, though."

Darbishire's letter read: *Dear Charles, I hope you are quite well. With love from Charles.*

"Better than nothing," he observed.

Jennings nodded. "I've been meaning to write to my Aunt Angela for the last three weeks, but I haven't got round to it yet. I think I'll do it now; it'll be something to make the envelope a bit fatter, and when it comes back to-morrow morning, I can bung it into another envelope and that'll be that."

The contents of Jennings's letters to his Aunt Angela were always based strictly on fact: yet they were worded in such a way that the reader was left with the impression that the writer was sparing no effort in helping the wheels of school routine to run more smoothly. This time, his letter said:

Dear Aunt Angela,

I meant to write to you before but I have been busy helping the Head to re-plant his roses in my spare time, and also useful work like rolling the cricket pitch.

The junior school went on a picnic but Darbishire and I went to a fête to help. It was very interesting. We helped a pig and gave Matron some bath salts. We have been doing a lot of things for the school, like, say, for instance we found some balls that had been lost and gave them to our friends, and everybody says I have a good chance of winning the sack race on Sports Day as I had some practice.

Darbishire had a headache but he is better now so I will close as I have no blotch, so can't turn over.

With love,
John.

At the end of the rest period they hurried downstairs and placed their stamped, addressed envelopes in the wire basket in the hall—the final act of a plan which had caused them so much trouble in its execution. On the morrow they would reap their reward: on the morrow they, alone, would be the proud possessors of the new *Scientific Inventions of the Twentieth Century* stamp, franked with the vital date, June 16th.

At five o'clock Robinson went into the hall to collect the letters for the evening post. The first two envelopes to catch his eye were addressed to J. C. T. Jennings and C. E. J. Darbishire at Linbury Court School.

There must be some mistake, somewhere, the cleaner decided. There was no point in spending good money sending letters through the post when the recipients were within a stone's throw of the posting-box.

He put the two envelopes aside. And later, after he

had returned from the village and the last post had gone, he gave them to Jennings as the boy was going indoors after evening break.

"Here you are! Letter for you and one for your friend," he said.

Jennings stared at the envelopes in dismay. No postmark—and too late to do anything about it!

"But they were meant for collection," he protested. "They were supposed to catch to-night's post."

"Didn't need posting. Waste of money," Robinson told him. "Besides, you've got them sooner this way, delivered by hand."

Jennings flipped his fingers with vexation. "You don't understand. These aren't just ordinary letters that somebody's sent us. Darbishire and I wrote them to ourselves."

"Wrote them to yourselves!" Robinson echoed in puzzled wonder. He was used to the fantastic antics of the younger generation, but this was something that didn't make sense whichever way he looked at it. "It's bad enough when you get people *talking* to themselves," he said severely. "But when it comes to people writing letters to themselves, it's time they had their brains tested."

Jennings didn't argue the point. He took the envelopes and wandered off to find Darbishire and tell him of the failure of their plan. It had been an odd sort of day, he thought, with the most unlikely people tipping the see-saw of their hopes up and down—Pettigrew, Mr. Wilkins, Miss Thorpe, Dr. Furnival—and now, to end it all, old Robo plunging the see-saw down with a wallop.

But what else could you expect, he asked himself, with people who wouldn't have recognized an exciting new issue of stamps, even if they'd had it served up on a plate with a sprig of holly on the top!

CHAPTER 13

# *The Squaw on the Hippo*

Mr. Carter strolled round the dining-hall during breakfast on Tuesday, handing out the letters which had arrived by the morning post. He reached the third-form table and looked with interest at one of the envelopes which he sorted out from the pile.

"Lucky old Jennings!" he remarked, handing the boy a letter. "Somebody's sent you one of those new stamps that came out yesterday."

Jennings could hardly believe his good fortune. The writing on the envelope was Aunt Angela's, and the stamp in the corner was legibly franked with the previous day's date. "Good old Aunt Angela!" he crowed, holding the letter up for everyone to see.

Immediately, there was a demand for a closer inspection, so the letter was passed unopened to the boys seated close at hand. Jennings refused to let it go farther afield. "You can all see it later on," he announced. "Darbi and I are going to hold a special exhibition in the tuck-box room after midday dinner."

"Admission free. Everybody welcome, but you've got to queue up without shoving," Darbishire added.

"Actually, it's a sheer fluke getting one of these with

the right postmark on," Jennings informed his fellow-breakfasters when the envelope was passed back, smeared with traces of bacon and marmalade. "My Aunt Angela hasn't a clue about stamps. She wouldn't have known there *was* a new issue yesterday, let alone queued up for it. I bet you what you like she just waltzed into a post office and had it given to her without asking."

Darbishire shook his head over his tea-cup. "Just like grown-ups," he observed in a voice tinged with envy. "Look at all the trouble we took to get ours franked—and then it didn't come off. Grown-ups get jam on everything."

"And we get marmalade," said Jennings, wiping the stains off with a scrap of dry bread. He opened the envelope and scanned the contents. "Nothing special," he reported. "She just wants to know why I haven't answered her last letter, so I'd better post her that one I wrote yesterday."

"You can't even do that now," Darbishire said gloomily. "You told me you'd sold your Aunt Angela's stamp to Miss Thorpe so you could buy one of the new ones: and you wouldn't want to waste one of *those* on a letter to an aunt, would you!"

It seemed that the letter to Aunt Angela was doomed—until Jennings remembered that Pettigrew was still in his debt to the amount of five pence in coppers. So after breakfast he added a note to Aunt Angela's letter while he waited for the day boy to arrive.

The postscript read:

Thank you for writing asking why I hadn't answered your letter, it is because I had to sell a person your old unused stamp to buy another unused new one, but as you have sent me a used new one I will get my money back from another person and buy an old unused one for your letter, so that will be all right.

Aunt Angela read the postscript through several times when she received her nephew's letter, but she never did understand what it meant.

While Jennings was busy in the common-room with his correspondence, Darbishire was listening to Mr. Wilkins, who had accosted him as he was walking past the staff room door.

"You missed my maths lesson yesterday morning when you were in the sick-room," the master was saying. "For your own sake I think you should try and catch up in your free time. Otherwise, you'll be all at sea when I go through the work in class this afternoon."

"Yes, sir. I shouldn't want to be all at sea, sir," the boy agreed.

"Right! Ask anyone in Form 3 to lend you his book, and copy out what I told them about the theorem of Pythagoras. And try to work out what it means. It's the sort of thing that's useful to know when you're marking out a tennis court or a football pitch!"

Darbishire wandered off to his classroom where the

only person present was Bromwich, who was hunting through his desk for a cricket ball.

"Hey, Bromo, will you lend me your maths notebook?" he asked. "Old Sir says I've got to copy out that work he showed you yesterday."

"That old thing about marking out tennis courts?" Bromwich foraged amongst his possessions and threw a notebook on to Darbishire's desk. "There you are! I hope you can read it. I had to take it down in rough because the bell went."

Darbishire opened the notebook and looked at the diagram. "Doesn't look like a tennis court to me—or a football pitch: more like a cock-eyed pile of old boxes. And anyway, you'd need whitewash or paint or something as well for marking them out, wouldn't you?"

"Sir didn't mean that. He meant—well, actually, I don't know what he meant because I wasn't listening. But you just copy it down from my book and you'll probably be able to work it out for yourself, if you're lucky."

Bromwich found his cricket ball and hurried from the room, leaving Darbishire to decipher the abbreviated squiggle. The scholar copied the diagram easily enough, but the writing underneath defeated him.

*In a rt angled △*, Bromwich had written, *the squar on the hippo=sum of the squars on the other 2 sides.*

What on earth did it mean? There was no such word as *squar*. Perhaps he meant squab? squad? squat? squaw?

The squaw on the hippo? In his mind's eye, Darbishire pictured the wife of a Red Indian chief, resplendent in feathered head-dress, riding proudly on the tribal hippopotamus.

But how could she be *equal* to the squaws on two other sides of the animal? Equal in weight? . . . In height? . . . In importance? He stared at the diagram wondering whether it was meant to represent a three-sided hippopotamus, but it wasn't easy to imagine what such an animal would look like in real life.

Determined to please Mr. Wilkins, he tried again. Perhaps the theorem meant that she was equal in weight. Supposing you had a very fat squaw, weighing, say, fifteen stone; and two thinner squaws sitting on the other side of the animal's back weighing say, eight stone and seven stone respectively . . . What then?

The scholar's eyes shone with inspiration. He'd got it! Seven and eight made fifteen! So the squaw on one side of the hippopotamus would be equal in weight to the sum of the squaws on the other two sides. That meant that the animal would be properly balanced and wouldn't topple over.

Funny subject—geometry, Darbishire reflected! He'd no idea you could work out problems like that with it. It was a bit confusing, at first, but anyone with a mathematical brain could see what Pythagoras was driving at! He copied down the wording beneath the diagram, convinced that Mr. Wilkins would be impressed with the progress his pupil had made by working in his spare time.

Shortly before afternoon school that day a small and

exclusive philatelic exhibition was held in the tuck-box room. There were only three stamps on show—one used and two unused specimens of the *Scientific Inventions of the Twentieth Century* series. All were attached to empty envelopes, one of which bore the authentic postmark of June 16th. The rarity of the exhibits called forth a great deal of envy and admiration.

"How about doing a swop, Jen?" Venables suggested. "I'll give you two of my new Italians for one of your unused two-and-a-half *p's*."

"Are you joking!" Jennings's tone was scornful. "They're worth a jolly sight more than your mouldy old new Italians."

"Well——" Venables searched his mind for some extra inducement. "I tell you what. I'll give you two packets of chewing-gum as well."

"Chewing-gum! Tut! Do me a favour!"

"Ah, but this is special top-quality, airline chewing-gum," Venables urged. "My uncle got it from the stewardess when he flew to New York. They give chewing-gum to all their passengers to stop their ears popping when the aircraft takes off."

Darbishire was interested. "How do they get it out of their ears when they get down to earth again?" he wanted to know.

Venables's offer was turned down, and the philatelists' reputation rode high as the spectators filed by the exhibits laid out on the window-sill. They were still filing by shortly after the bell had rung for afternoon school; and Mr. Wilkins, who happened to be passing the door on the way to his classroom, came in to find out what was going on.

"What on earth are you boys doing down here in the tuck-box room!" he barked. "The bell went two minutes ago. Upstairs, quickly, to your classrooms."

There was a rush to leave the room, but Jennings and Darbishire were reluctant to go without their stamps. Unfortunately, Mr. Wilkins had come to rest by the window, cutting off the exhibitors from their exhibits, and it was impossible for them to reach their property without pushing past him.

"Run along, you two. Sharpish, now. You heard what I said!"

"Oh, but sir, I just want to get something," Jennings pleaded.

"No time! We've got a lot of work to get through this lesson," Mr. Wilkins retorted. "It will have to wait until after school, whatever it is."

"Oh, but sir, it's a rare stamp exhibition."

"I've no doubt it is, but it won't come to any harm. Nobody's going to steal it, and stamps can't walk."

Jennings's protests were over-ruled. The stamped envelopes were left to take their chance on the window-sill and the boys were chivvied upstairs to Classroom 3.

Darbishire was rather looking forward to the maths lesson. He had taken a great deal of trouble in studying the theorem of Pythagoras in his spare time and was anxious to display his knowledge.

On the blackboard Mr. Wilkins drew a right-angled

triangle and constructed squares on the hypotenuse and on the other two sides.

"Now, I know I didn't have time to explain this properly last lesson," he reminded the class. "But I told you to bring your brains to bear on the subject during prep and see what you could work out for yourselves." He looked hopefully along the front row for a volunteer to spring to his feet and explain the Pythagorean proposition.

He was disappointed! Temple said it still looked like a lop-sided windmill to him, and Bromwich added that he thought it was something to do with getting the corners straight on a football pitch, but he wouldn't commit himself further.

Mr. Wilkins was about to admit defeat when he noticed a hand flapping like a tea-towel on a clothes line to attract his attention. "Well, Darbishire, were you able to work out for yourself the significance of the square on the hypotenuse?"

"Yes, I think so, sir, though it's a bit tricky," the mathematician replied. "So far as I can make out it's to do with spreading the load, so you don't get too much weight in one place."

Mr. Wilkins was puzzled. "Go on," he said, guardedly.

"Well, sir, supposing you had a Red Indian chief with three wives and he wanted to take them on a journey. According to Pythagoras, he'd have to put the fat one up at the front and the two skinny ones down by its tail so that the hippopotamus wouldn't over-balance." Darbishire paused and frowned importantly. "But I still don't see how that helps you to mark out a tennis court!"

There was a baffled silence after Darbishire had finished his explanation of the theorem of Pythagoras. His colleagues stared at him blankly. Mr. Wilkins just sat quietly with his head in his hands, wondering why he bothered to go on trying to teach mathematics to Form 3. There must be easier ways of earning a living, he thought!

It took until the end of the lesson to convince Darbishire that the proposition had nothing to do with squaws on hippopotamuses (and even this led to an argument as to whether the plural of the word shouldn't be *hippopotami*). But eventually he admitted that he might, perhaps, have been misled by Bromwich's abbreviations.

Even so, he was reluctant to abandon his theory altogether because it sounded so plausible.

"This chap, Pythagoras, sir; how long ago did he live?" he asked Mr. Wilkins just before the end of the lesson.

Mr. Wilkins considered. "H'm! About two thousand five hundred years ago, roughly."

"Well, there you are, sir!" Darbishire's tone was triumphant. "They hadn't even *invented* football in those days, so how could Pythagoras have worked out a method for marking out the pitch!"

* * * *

As soon as school was over, Jennings and Darbishire hurried down to the tuck-box room to retrieve their stamps.

To their dismay, they couldn't get in. Robinson was sweeping the room, and the school cleaner had devised a foolproof method of ensuring that he was not disturbed by boys while carrying out his duties. He always locked the door, so saving himself from being pestered by questions and followed round by dirty footmarks.

"It's no good. He won't let us in. He never does," Darbishire said when Jennings's frantic pounding on the door panels produced no result. "We'll have to leave it till after cricket. Old Robo will probably look after the stamps for us when he finds them. He's quite decent, usually, about that sort of thing."

Frustrated, they went off to get ready for cricket; and when they came in again just before tea they found the tuck-box room swept and dusted—but no trace of stamped envelopes on the window-sill.

"Where's old Robo? We must find him at once!" Jennings cried in alarm.

"You'll be lucky! He's gone down to the village with the post," said Rumbelow, who was foraging through his tuck-box. "I saw him hoofing off when I was umpiring."

This was a set-back, but not necessarily a disaster. "We'll have to see him after tea, then," Jennings decided. "Keep your fingers crossed, Darbi. Let's hope he's put them in a safe place."

There was still no sign of Robinson when the meal was over, for after his return from the village the odd-job man retired to his cottage for a well-earned rest. He emerged again after evening preparation, just as the boys were going out on to the games field for their last hour of freedom before the dormitory bell.

Jennings ran him to earth in the tool-shed and embarked at once on the reason for his visit.

"Excuse me, but you know when you were doing the tuck-box room this afternoon," the boy began. "Did you find three envelopes on the window-sill?"

Robinson nodded and laid down the chisel he was sharpening. "That's right. Two of them looked like the same ones I gave back to you last night."

"Yes, they were. Thank goodness they're safe. Where did you put them, please?"

From his jacket hanging on the back of the door, Robinson produced two envelopes and pointed to the unused stamps affixed to them. "Still worth two-and-a-half *p* each, these are," he said. "Haven't been through the post, see, so you can steam them off and use them again."

"Ah, but these are for our stamp albums. We shan't be putting them on letters, now we've missed getting the postmark we wanted." Jennings took the envelopes, put them in his pocket and stood waiting expectantly. "And where's the other one?" he asked.

"The other one?" Robinson looked puzzled. "Wasn't any point in saving an old envelope, seeing as how it had been used already." He turned back to his work bench. "I threw it away, along with the rest of the rubbish."

Jennings stared at him in wide-eyed dismay. "But that was the most valuable one of the lot," he cried. "It was the only one we'd got with the proper day-of-issue franking on it."

Mr. Henry Robinson—like Miss Thorpe and like Pettigrew—was no philatelist. "Well, how was I to know that!" he defended himself. He picked up his chisel and started to sharpen it. Then, rather grudgingly, he went on: "Well, if it's all that important you'd better go and have a look on my bonfire: I've only just put a match to it. Wind's blowing from the south-west, so there's a chance to-day's rubbish won't get burnt up for an hour or so, yet."

CHAPTER 14

# *Full Circle*

JENNINGS TORE OUT of the tool-shed and raced off towards the patch of waste ground behind the greenhouse where Robinson burnt the rubbish. On the way he passed a group of third-formers setting out on an expedition to collect fresh leaves for their caterpillars.

"To the bonfire! . . . To the bonfire! . . ." he cried dramatically and pointed the way ahead. "Emergency *red*! All hands to the pump! Find Darbishire, somebody, and tell him to come!"

His tone was so urgent that the caterpillar caterers abandoned their foraging and followed, agog with curiosity. Skirting the forbidden territory of the kitchen garden, they ran down the path to the junction by the potting-shed where the track branched off towards the rear entrance of the school grounds. On the left was a greenhouse and a cluster of outbuildings, beyond which a few wispy spirals of smoke indicated the site of the odd-job man's weekly bonfire.

Jennings arrived some distance ahead of the others. He stopped for a moment and glanced round, wondering where to begin his search.

Only by a stretch of the imagination could Robinson's never-ending struggle with the combustible rubbish of Linbury Court School be called a proper bonfire. More often than not, the fire was no more than a sprawling rubbish heap upon which the debris of the waste-paper baskets was strewn and left to take its chance of survival. Sometimes it burned, sometimes it didn't: and as more rubbish was heaped upon the top, the lower layers disintegrated into a slightly-scorched compost which grew deeper as the term wore on. It was only during the holidays that Robinson really got down to the task of clearing the site with a roaring fire in readiness for the refuse of the following term.

Jennings rushed to the nearest spiral of smoke and was gingerly spreading out the embers with the toe of his shoe when the rest of the group came pounding up behind him.

"What's all the hoo-hah?" Martin-Jones demanded.

"My envelope with the special stamp on. It's been thrown away." At least three separate fires were smouldering on the rubbish tip and Jennings exhorted his helpers to waste no time. "I'll have a look through this one. You lot split up and go and tackle the others. And search through all the stuff that *isn't* burning, too. It might be anywhere."

The helpers knew what they were looking for, as they had attended the exclusive stamp exhibition earlier in the day. So they spread out over the site, stirring up the compost with sticks, kicking over the ashes and raking out the fires with any implement that came to hand.

Darbishire arrived soon afterwards, having heard a rumour that something sensational was afoot. He raced up to Jennings who was wading about ankle-deep in the remains of some half-burnt cornflake packets. "What's happened?" he squawked.

Jennings pointed vaguely at the charred remains. "Old Robo. He's thrown our stamp away."

"Coo! Treacherous traitor!" Darbishire fumed.

"It wasn't sabotage—just ignorance," Jennings explained. "He couldn't see why anyone should want to hang on to an old envelope they couldn't use again. You'd better start looking: it's bound to be lying about somewhere, if it hasn't been burned already."

They searched round the rim of the fire, poking the rotting cartons and turning up lumps of shapeless salvage. For a while the quest seemed hopeless: and then, just as he was digging his way down to a deeper layer of wastepaper, Jennings saw Aunt Angela's handwriting on an envelope untouched by the flames.

"Hooray! Success! Success!' he shouted, waving the scrap of paper in the air. "You can all stop looking now—I've found it."

Some of the searchers straightened up and brushed the dirt and ashes from their socks and shoes: but others, like beachcombers on the seashore, were filled with an urge to carry on scavenging in the hope that unexpected treasure lay buried beneath their feet.

Atkinson found a mini cement lorry belonging to Rumbelow: Bromwich found Temple's long lost magnifying glass and Martin-Jones found three pieces of Binns's and Blotwell's abandoned jigsaw puzzle.

But it was Venables who made the most interesting discovery. Six inches below the surface he found a small sack which, after a struggle, he managed to pull clear. He wrinkled his nose in puzzled surprise, for the sack was stuffed full of soft round objects which he thought at first were old potatoes.

"Hey! Roll up and inspect ye pirates' treasure," he cried. "Stand by for ye fabulous unveiling ceremony." He tipped the sack upside down, but instead of potatoes, old tennis balls and cork cricket balls came rolling out.

"Know what these are?" he asked his fellow-scavengers. "These are the old balls Jen and Darbi bunged down from the gym roof, that time."

"That's right," Martin-Jones confirmed. "Old Wilkie said he was going to throw away all the ones he confiscated—and here they are."

Temple picked one up. "This is the one I hit up off old Darbi's bowling," he said proudly. "Remember our famous test match—The World *versus* Outer Space? We didn't get far with *that* fixture, did we!"

"We could go on with it now, if we wanted to," Atkinson suggested. "At least, we've got some spare balls in case of accidents."

Jennings was feeling light-hearted again now that the three stamped envelopes were safely in his blazer pocket.

"Come on, then! Outer Space challenges the Earth!"

he cried in ringing tones. "Same teams as before. We'll go on from Darbi bowling to Temple, just where we left off."

There was still more than half an hour's free time left before the end of evening break, so Venables picked up the rotting sack and the boys hurried off to the tarmac pitch outside the gymnasium.

The chalked wicket was still on the wall of the bicycle shed. At the other end of the pitch a blazer was flung down to mark the bowling crease. Temple strode to the wicket with his old, worn bat, the fielders took their places and the game began.

The first ball that Darbishire sent down was an easy long-hop on the leg. The batsman stepped out and smote it with all his strength. It soared over the heads of the fielders, struck the parapet above the gymnasium and rolled to rest on the roof.

"Boundary six! Well done, Earth!" Temple said with satisfaction. He grinned at the captain of the opposing side. "Hey, Jennings, how about you and Darbi going up on the roof and fagging it."

"No jolly fear," said the man from Mars.

"That's what you did last time."

"Yes, and look what it led to!" Jennings pulled a face as the chain of events flashed through his mind. If they hadn't gone up to the roof, he would never have been trapped in the sleeping-bag. If he hadn't been caught in the bag, he wouldn't have been in detention for the picnic. If he hadn't been in detention, he wouldn't have won the pig. If he hadn't won the pig, he wouldn't have had to roll the cricket square. If he hadn't done that he might have written sooner to Aunt Angela. So he wouldn't have had a letter from her that morning. So Robinson wouldn't have thrown the envelope on the rubbish heap. And if they hadn't been searching the rubbish they wouldn't have found the balls for the test match, thus enabling Temple to hit the ball on the roof again!

"We're back where we started," Jennings said. "Leave the old ball where it is. We've got plenty more to be going on with."

But when the game was re-started, the balls were found to be a problem. Months of lying on the roof, followed by a further four weeks at the bottom of the rubbish heap, had reduced them to such a state of disintegration that one good hit was enough to send the core flying one way and the outer skin flying another.

The composition cricket balls were the least reliable: some broke in half on impact with the bat: others split into fragments in mid-air, scattering like splinters from a nuclear rocket re-entering the earth's atmosphere. The tennis balls were more durable and managed to survive longer, but even so they had no bounce and had to be bowled full-pitch in order to reach the batsman.

In these conditions it was no wonder that the opening batsman for the All-World XI had an innings of varying luck. In his second over he survived being caught by Atkinson because the ball fell to pieces in the fielder's hands. But shortly afterwards he was out *L.B.W.* to an egg-shaped plastic object which burst with a loud report when it hit him on the shin.

"This is hopeless," Venables complained, when he had finished laughing at Temple's discomfiture. "We can't go on like this, Jen. We'll have to change the rules."

"Why not," Darbishire agreed. "After all, we're supposed to be a touring team from Space and for all anyone knows the laws of cricket are quite different on Pluto and places." He frowned in thought, probing the possibilities of the idea. "Supposing, say, for instance, there was no gravity on the planet you came from. Okay, then, when you hit the ball up in the air it wouldn't come down again, would it!"

"Just like ours don't when we hit them on the gym roof," said Jennings. His eyes lit up with inspiration. "That's what we could do, then! Test Match according to Outer Space rules! Everything's opposite from what it is on Earth, and you can only score runs by hitting the ball into orbit so it doesn't come back!"

Nobody had the slightest idea of what Jennings was talking about, and it took him a few minutes to explain how the laws of non-gravity cricket differed from those of the M.C.C.

Instead of scoring runs, he told them, the object of the game was to lose as many balls as possible, by sending them on a one-way journey into space. Using the flat roof of the gymnasium as a substitute for a non-gravitational field, the batsman must try to hit the balls over the parapet to the place whence they had come.

To achieve this, bowler and batsman must work in partnership instead of being on opposing sides. A ball lost on the roof entitled the partners to have another go. When they failed, their places must be taken by the next pair in the line.

"All it means, really, is hitting sixes off the pottiest bowling in history," the advocate of the New Laws finished up. "Let's start, anyway, and make up any more rules we need as we go along."

* * * *

Mr. Carter and Mr. Wilkins were taking a stroll round the grounds during the hour before the dormitory bell. The weather was warm with the prospect of another fine day to follow, and on all sides there were signs that boys and masters of Linbury Court School were making good use of the evening break.

Mr. Hind was coaching a group on the tennis courts, the headmaster was bowling at the First XI nets. Over by the pavilion Paterson was oiling his bat, Thompson was practising the guitar, and Binns and Blotwell were laying out a brand new five-hundred-piece jigsaw puzzle on a square of hardboard.

But despite all this purposeful activity, Mr. Wilkins's mood was sombre, and he was holding forth in gloomy tones on a subject which was seldom far from his mind.

"Yes, I dare say, Carter, but it's those boys in Form 3—and Jennings, in particular—who are the real problem," he was complaining as they crossed the quad. "No sense of responsibility! When you think that in a few years' time those silly little boys will be out in the world earning their living or training for careers, it's enough to make your mind boggle with apprehension."

He paused for a moment to let his mind boggle. When it had boggled to a stop, he went on: "Take Darbishire, for instance. He told me the other day that he wants to be a scientist when he grows up. How in the name of reason can you make a scientist out of a boy who thinks that the square on the hypotenuse is something to do with a Red Indian riding on a rhinocerous—or some such twaddle!"

At that moment, shouts of laughter and cheers of triumph came wafting across the quad from the playground beside the gymnasium.

Mr. Carter raised an enquiring eyebrow. "Sounds like a celebration!"

"Sounds like a riot, if you ask me," his colleague retorted. "We'd better go and see what they're up to, I suppose."

When the masters reached the makeshift cricket pitch by the bicycle shed, they found a group of third-formers gathered in a circle. From the knees downwards they were caked in ash from the bonfire site, and most of them had a similar grey deposit on their hands and faces.

On the edge of the circle Venables stood with a little pile of balls at his feet and a filthy old potato sack slung across his shoulders. In the centre, Jennings with a cricket bat faced Darbishire holding a perished rubber ball.

As the masters approached, the bowler lobbed the ball gently towards the batsman who took aim and smote it up into the air as high as the gymnasium building. The ball struck the parapet with a spongy *plop* like an over-ripe grapefruit, broke into pieces and rolled out of sight on to the roof.

Another volley of cheers rang out from the ash-stained group. "Hooray! . . . Boundary six for Mars and Pluto . . . Another Flying Object off the launching-pad!"

Mr. Wilkins led the way into the circle. "What in the name of thunder are you boys playing at?" he demanded.

Jennings faced the masters with a smile of welcome. "Oh, hullo, sir! We're playing cricket."

"Playing *what*!" Mr. Wilkins, a keen sportsman, was appalled by this outrageous travesty of the game. "You don't call this *cricket*, do you!"

"We're playing under the new Inter-planetary rules, sir. Specially made up for test matches in the Solar System and places where there isn't any gravity," the boy explained. "Of course, they haven't actually been passed by the M.C.C. yet," he conceded.

Darbishire stepped forward to fill in a few details. "The balls are Unidentified Flying Objects and the gym roof is outer space, you see, sir," he said. "And instead of scoring in the ordinary way, you have to launch the objects into orbit so they never come back."

"Sounds an expensive game," Mr. Carter observed, puffing at his pipe. "The cost in new balls must be considerable."

"Ah, yes, it might be for some people, sir. But we're lucky because we've got our own special private supply of disposable flying objects."

Mr. Wilkins's glance travelled round the group of dishevelled space-cricketers and came to rest on the disposable flying objects at Venables's feet. He frowned and said: "Aren't those the balls I confiscated a month ago? Who told you boys you could have them? You'd no right to touch them!"

The players shifted their feet uncomfortably, and once again the explanation was left to Jennings. "Well, you see, sir, we were just trying to carry out your wishes."

Mr. Wilkins was baffled. "My *wishes*!"

"Yes, in a way, sir. You see, I remembered that when Darbishire and I—sort of—absentmindedly threw them all down from the roof that time, you'd sounded a bit—er—well a bit annoyed at what we'd done," Jennings explained with a look of starry-eyed innocence on his face. "So when we happened to find them lying on the rubbish heap and making it look untidy, we thought we'd do you a favour by sending them all back again where they'd come from. We thought you'd appreciate it, sir."

"*Doh!* You silly little boys! I've never in all my life heard such a fantastic——"

The tirade was interrupted by Mr. Hind's whistle sounding the end of evening break. "Take the rest of those balls back to the bonfire and then go and make yourselves tidy," Mr. Wilkins barked. "You're not going into the dining-hall for supper looking like a bunch of scarecrows."

So ended the first (and only) Test Match played according to the new Inter-planetary rules between human beings and their counterparts from beyond the radiation belts.

The visitors from Jupiter, Venus, Pluto and Mars brushed themselves down and trotted off with their Earthbound opponents for a glass of milk and a biscuit before the dormitory bell.

Mr. Wilkins shook his head in despair as he watched them go. "Doesn't that prove what I was saying just now about boys in Form 3 and Jennings, in particular," he said to his colleague as the little group disappeared round the corner of the main building. "We send them out on to the playing-field to practise cricket; and instead of trying to improve their game, they reduce the whole process to a pantomime of monumental lunacy."

"They'll grow out of it," Mr. Carter assured him.

"I hope you're right, Carter, but I see precious little sign of it at the moment." Mr. Wilkins heaved a deep and exasperated sigh. His mind had started to boggle again! "What's going to happen in a few years' time, when, instead of being sent out on to the playing-field, they're sent out into the world!"

Mr. Carter re-lit his pipe. "Don't worry, Wilkins," he said calmly. "Even third-formers grow up to be people!"